MW00622886

Dreaming a World

Dreaming a World

Korean Birth Mothers Tell Their Stories

edited by Sangsoon Han, director of Ae Ran Won

Yeong & Yeong Book Company

Dreaming a World: Korean Birth Mothers Tell Their Stories

Yeong & Yeong Book Company
St. Paul, Minnesota

www.yeongandyeong.com

© 2010 by Yeong & Yeong Book Company
All rights reserved. No part of this book may be reproduced, scanned, or distributed in any printed or electronic form without permission. Please do not participate in or encourage piracy of copyrighted materials in violation of the authors' rights.

Interior design and typesetting: Stephanie Billecke
Cover design: Ann Delgehausen, Trio Bookworks
Front jacket painting and interior art © Hyun Kyu Lim

Cataloging-in-Publication data is on file at the Library of Congress, http://catalog.loc.gov.

ISBN: 978-1-59743-001-2

Printed in Canada
15 14 13 12 11 10   1 2 3 4 5

This book is printed on acid-free paper.

Except where noted, all names and identifying details in this book have been changed to protect the privacy of the writers.

To My Dear Baby

To my dear baby
To give you your life
I suffered all the pain in the world
I was deserted by my parents and your father
After much labor pains
Eventually you saw the light of the world

But
Now that I do not have anything to give you
I am frustrated and in pain to see myself so helpless
Sending you away for the happiness that I cannot give
I hate myself for sending you to the faraway land.

My dear baby
The only thing I can do for you
Is to cry, love and pray
I can only pray because I care for you
For I can, at least, pray for you
I am suffering but happy.

Dear Baby
Hope you will be happy, healthy and bright
Remember that is your birth mother's only wish.
I will not forget you till the end of my life
With the belief that the child you pray for will not fail
I will not stop praying for you until my death.
"God! Please fulfill my wish."

I love you, forever and ever.

—Mom, who loves you—

Introduction

After the publication of *I Wish for You a Beautiful Life,* I received letters from many Koreans who had been adopted overseas. Having read that book, many of these adoptees wanted to visit Ae Ran Won, and a lot of them have actually now done so. They said, "I could not read this book without tears, but I was pleased to know about the love of my birth mother, who had given me up. But why? I was not able to find the answer about why she had to send me away. I want to know that."

I delivered this feedback to birth mothers who had joined an Ae Ran Won self-help group after moving out of our facility. These were not the birth mothers of those specific adoptees, but we discussed how the circumstances of Korean unwed mothers are often quite similar, and we wondered if it would be good to talk and write about the reasons they had to send their children, whom they loved, to be adopted abroad.

I met Dr. Sook Wilkinson in Minnesota in 2003. She is the co-editor of the book *After the Morning Calm: Reflections of Korean Adoptees.* She said, "*After the Morning Calm* is full of adoptees' life stories from the time they arrived in America. I hope that at some time a prequel—the story up to when Korean birth mothers sent their children abroad— will be published." I said that Ae Ran Won and Korean birth mothers would try to provide that part of the story. When I returned to Ae Ran Won, I delivered Sook Wilkinson's message to the birth mothers in our programs.

They all agreed, but asked for more information about what the adoptees wanted to know.

Since then, I have asked adoptees whom I've met to share their thoughts about what they would hope to learn from a book of birth mothers' stories. When I relayed these discussions to the birth mothers, they felt positive about it. One birth mother commented, "If it helps adoptees, I would gladly open up my wounded past." Another said, "I don't know whether my child will read this or not, but if someone is helped from this writing, when my birth child needs help, someone around him may lend a hand." I put a notice on the homepage of Ae Ran Won, inviting members to participate, and, with an attitude geared to sharing and healing, birth mothers started writing their stories as if they were opening up in front of their children.

As they wrote, some of their families criticized them. "You should not be proud of what you have done." "Why would you want to let the whole world find out about it?" "Aren't you ashamed of yourself at all?" However, they never gave up on telling their stories, and they willingly accepted the criticism. The mothers thought that this was the one thing they could do, as birth mothers who had not been able to raise their own children, to ease the pain and curiosity of adoptees who are longing to understand why some birth mothers had to choose adoption.

It was not easy for these women to put into writing what they had in mind. They had to write honestly about them-selves while being continually reminded of painful memo-ries. They had to re-experience the pain, the helplessness, and the loss they had been trying to conceal. They often had to call me, and some cried again and again as the feeling of emptiness that had been buried in their hearts floated up into consciousness and became hard to bear. Sometimes they were captured by shock and chaos as painful memories vividly flashed back. Then they rushed to hold onto me and could do nothing but cry. The act of sending their children away may have been "in the past," but it was simultaneously "present" for each mother. These feelings surged constantly as they wrote their stories, line by line. This book would not have been possible without all the pain that the birth mothers endured, but it gives them huge pleasure to have shared these stories for the sake of their children.

There have been slight changes in Korea's patriarchal culture. Previously, the human rights of unmarried mothers and their children were not acknowledged. Any pregnancy before marriage, even if caused by rape, was never acceptable. The pregnant woman was considered to be lucky if the perpetrator decided to have mercy and take care of her.

Until recently, people considered abortion to be a solution to pregnancy before marriage. Some people have visited me at Ae Ran Won and asserted, "If these girls were your daughters, would you still let them give a birth? If you really want to help them, persuade them all to have abortions, and send them back home." However, public awareness of the seriousness of Korea's low birthrate has influenced the general acceptance of pregnancy and childbirth. Some people have encouraged me, saying, "You are doing an important job saving lives," and observing that sometimes "even married couples hesitate to take charge of their own children when they get divorced; it is great that an unmarried mother is willing to raise a child alone."

As the Korean National Assembly and the Government revised the Single Mother-Child Welfare Act in December, 2006, an amendment clearly stated that facilities may support unmarried mothers who request support in order to raise their children. However, no budget is allocated solely for this purpose. As a result, only a few of the more than forty maternity homes in South Korea have made space for unmarried mothers and their babies, and supported, through fund-raising, the mothers who keep their babies.

At the same time, the number of unmarried mothers who want to raise their children has been rising, and these mothers need support facilities. Since 1999, Ae Ran Won has been developing such a support system. According to statistics for 2008, 80% of unmarried mothers who entered Ae Ran Won decided to raise their children themselves. That percentage will increase even more in coming years. By contrast, only 1% did so in 1995, and by the year 2000 about 20% of the unmarried mothers kept their babies. The increase over the years was mostly because Ae Ran Won opened group homes for these mothers, and found other means of support, which gave more women the option to keep their babies. Ae Ran Won had previously supported unmarried mothers, from 1989 to 1994. At that time, the outside nursery took care of children three years and older, so Ae Ran Won had to build an inside nursery to take care of the babies, while supporting the mothers with vocational training. This program was shut down in July 1994 by an administrative order of the Seoul City government, which did not then understand why Ae Ran Won wanted to support unmarried mothers in keeping their babies.

Clearly, many challenges remain. The Ministry of Health, Welfare, and Family is currently establishing comprehensive policies for unmarried mothers and making a roadmap for further assistance of birth mothers' sustenance and child rearing. Similar plans launched by the Ministry of Female and Family were abrogated because the budget was not secured in advance, which left harsh memories with those who fought for these plans. Needless to say, we should first secure the budget to put these plans into effect.

There are as yet no social support systems in Korea other than the facilities for unwed single-parent families. Single mothers are able to receive assistance only if they enter one of the fifteen unmarried single mothers' group homes in the nation. However, the amount of housing is insufficient compared to the number of the mothers who are raising their children. If an unmarried mother fails to be admitted to a group home, then she is on her own.

Unmarried single mothers can receive 50,000 won per month for child rearing as social welfare aid from the government. However, most of them give this up because each would have to reveal the fact that she is an unmarried single mother in front of local officials and make them understand her situation. In addition, the government limits this aid, giving it only to those mothers whose monthly income is very low, and ending the support when the child is ten years old.

The unwed mother has to face her local community's inhospitality without preparation, even though she needs help desperately. In this situation, mothers get worn out by the struggle to care for their babies and themselves, and sometimes give up on motherhood and even life itself. The result, as indicated by statistics from the Child Abuse Prevention Center: abuse, abandonment, and relinquishment of children.

In 2006 Ae Ran Won established the Me.You.Us. Support Center, an unwed single mothers' support center that helps women even if they are outside established facilities. Now the service helps women become more self-reliant in addition to assisting with child-rearing concerns. I am hopeful that this model will secure a position in a new paradigm of seeing to the welfare of Korean unwed single mothers and their children.

I am grateful to all of the people who helped to get this book published.

More than anything else, I appreciate the many birth mothers who answered the question "Why?" by opening up and sharing their painful pasts. After writing, many of the birth mothers said things like, "I am really relieved now because, even if I were to die suddenly, my child could learn from this book why I had to decide on adoption." They are now waiting for any response from the book's readers.

I sincerely thank Mr. Brian Boyd, who donated all the proceeds from publishing *I Wish for You a Beautiful Life* to Ae

Ran Won. The proceeds developed into a fund that became the seed money for a group home. He has promised to publish this book under the same conditions. The proceeds of this book will be used to assist unmarried single mothers who are having difficulties in their local communities, and for the social, psychological, and financial support of unmarried mothers and their children. I deeply appreciate Brian Boyd.

Thanks to Ms. Hyun Kyu Lim, an artist who contributed her precious paintings and changed Ae Ran Won into a nice place like an elegant gallery, and who has supported the unmarried mothers' child rearing efforts. I deeply appreciate that she has permitted the use of these paintings in this book for free.

I also thank Ross Oke, who was in charge of translation coordination and proof reading, Hyenah Seo, Hana Schneider, and my daughter, Joo Yun Jun, who participated in translation, and Soyoung Park at Brown University for the final proof reading. I appreciate that this book could see the light thanks to the efforts of all these people.

I would like to mention that, as in *I Wish for You a Beautiful Life,* you can find that many birth mothers process their experiences with the help of Christian concepts and words. Some of these expressions translate better than others, but they can help us understand the birth mothers' deep feelings of self-blame and guilt related to being unable to keep their children. Like the sense of urgency a person who is drowning must feel, the sense of powerlessness felt by mothers who have to send their children away leads them to pursue the absolute being. Many of them take the view that

"If there is an absolute being, I sincerely hope that He takes care of my baby." At the same time, some birth mothers develop strong religious belief systems that are important aspects of their worldview and manner of coping with loss.

At Ae Ran Won we are keenly aware of the undeniable fact that human beings are not complete figures, and we deeply respect the many and varied approaches that birth mothers take to working through their experiences. It is my great hope that people will learn to live together in harmonious society rather than criticize others who do not match their own standards or outlook.

Ae Ran Won has established a support system for unwed mothers and children, and developed the system to assist them more effectively. I hope all these little efforts bear fruit to promote public awareness regarding the human rights and welfare of unwed mothers and their children. We hope a good result will come out for more concern and support from the government and from the society. I hope Korean society will consider the children of unwed mothers as equal to any other children. I think it can be approved by establishing related laws and regulations to hold the birth fathers also responsible. The unwed mothers should not solely be blamed.

Finally, I would like to close by presenting a poem by South Korean poet Keun Bae Lee.

On the Road Ahead

On the road ahead,
There is a time we fall down,
when we are not supposed to.

On the road ahead,
There is a time we say love,
when we are not supposed to say it.

On the road ahead,
There is a time we show our tears,
when we are not supposed to show them.

On the road ahead,
There is a time we should send a loving person not to love.
There is a time we send a thing we should not send,
and live as a beast being locked in the dark,
on the road ahead.

chapter 1

After Long and Tormenting Prayer

(baby born in 1984)

I've never wanted to remember the time when I was young, because my family was so poor. There are six in my family: me, a brother, two sisters (one older than me and one who is younger), my mother and my very old father. I was easygoing and had so much *jung,* warm-hearted affection, that I would often go out of my way to help friends. My heart ached and I cried when I saw someone in pain. I had a soft spot for the suffering of others. I started working as a housemaid to get money for my younger sister and to make a financial contribution to the family. I liked to read and I became my teacher's favorite, maybe because of that. One day I was ordered to the teachers' office and was given a book. I thought my teacher must have told the schoolmaster about me. Before I knew it, I was hired as a housemaid for the married daughter of the schoolmaster.

I was fourteen at the time, and the house in my care was big. Once I noticed my hands were frostbitten, swollen, cracked, and later runny from an infection. But I was determined to work hard and pay the tuition for my sister who was at the time in her junior high school years. I bought household items for my family. I was beginning to wear the pants in my family.

After that I started at a new job as a clerk at a sports equipment store. One day I was returning by taxi from the shop's supplier in Dongdaemun East Gate Market. The taxi driver had been glancing at me in the rearview mirror during the ride. After a while, he stopped the cab in some woods I'd never seen before. He raped me there. Later, he finally spoke to me. He asked me to forgive him and said he liked me so much that he insisted that I should live with him. He had two sons who were seven and five years old. He kept saying that I should be their mother. He forced me into a *yogwan* hotel and had me stay there. He commuted to the taxi company until he realized that he was spending all his earnings on food and lodging. So he took me to his sister's house and got me pregnant. I was five foot four inches tall and weighed only ninety-five pounds. I was very thin. At the age of twenty-one, I was forced to become a mother of two children whose father I didn't love.

My pregnancy made my situation more complicated. Strangely, I was finding joy in being pregnant, as if I were normal like other women. But at the same time I was forced to live as a lover. I thought it was my karma, but this drastic change also made me feel depressed in an unfathomable way. I had terrible morning sickness and I lost weight, weighing only eighty-two pounds during the pregnancy. Despite my difficulties in keeping down food, I did all the household chores. My stomach turned even with a sip of water. My so-called in-laws had been married for ten years, but had not been successful in having their own child. The sister-in-law would keep herself busy with church work for the rest of the day after her husband left for work. I felt embarrassed that I was pregnant because of what they might have felt about the situation. My husband must have felt secure in the fact that he got me pregnant; he expressed his joy and begged me to give him a daughter.

I did take good care of his sons, but they were crying for their mother at night. Their father must have felt sad about this, and he searched for their mother while he was working. Finally he found her, and he told me that he didn't need me. He took me home. He told me to wait, and came for a visit once a week, and then the number of his visits dwindled to maybe once a month. My mother and father heaved a deep, sad sigh whenever they thought of the fate I was facing in my prime years. My brother said I should go somewhere else and kill myself, and my sister expressed the shame she believed I brought to the family. One day I fell asleep with the book I was reading on my stomach, and the book fell off, waking me. Ah! I felt mysterious joy and happiness at the movements inside me. My home was located in a rural town with a total of thirty homes. As I grew big with the baby, the neighbors started to throw me very uncomfortable glances.

My due date was imminent. By then I was a nervous wreck, hoping my man would show up on the doorstep at any moment. I didn't still have any plan for the future. One day he did appear but broke the news that he had reunited with his wife. I felt as if the earth jolted at the news. I cried and cried. What would ever become of me and the infant inside me! He promised to come and get me when he was able to rent a place, and then he left. But I could not believe his promise. I was twenty-one, and the situation was simply unbearable to handle by myself.

Three days before my due date, I called a phone number I came across in a women's magazine. I was directed to Ae Ran Won, where I found comfort in being with girls in a situation similar to mine. The program at Ae Ran Won, the church service and the disciplined schedule had all the elements needed to cheer me up in my depression and pregnancy. Before arriving there, I had begged my mother to raise the baby like her own. I would work hard and make enough money. I thought I would never have to give up the baby. I would just live for the baby, and I would never marry! My mother had taken this all in stride and shed tears of deep sadness. I realized what I did to my mother. I broke my mother's heart. Oh, I felt terrible.

Then, God took pity on me and guided me here to this wonderful place. I did the right thing to come here. After long and tormented prayer, I decided to go ahead with an adoption for my baby. I wanted her to live without the label of a fatherless child. Instead of this helpless and unmarried mother, my baby would have capable and caring parents. I believed they would raise her well, and she would go to college. My baby would have all the support she would need. Maybe I was trading my unrealistic ambition for the future of the baby.

"My little princess," I prayed, "I can't put you through the misery you and I were thrown into, because of my foolishness. I choose adoption for your own sake. But, my little baby, I will never stop praying for your happiness."

My labor started at eight o'clock on a Saturday night. I was taken to the clinic along with my roommate. The two attendants at the clinic said the delivery would not take place until morning, and they went back to their quarters. Soon my roommate returned to her bedroom, too. I was kept in the delivery room all by myself. I paced the room with bare feet, hungry and thirsty. The pain in my stomach and waist was very severe, but there was nobody to turn to for comfort. The labor continued until morning, when I gave birth to a daughter at 7:05. I reached to touch her cheek. She turned her face as if she knew I was about to nurse her. I still remember the moment so clearly. A moment later, the baby was taken from me, by a woman from the adoption agency. I felt numb and hopeless. Why can't you just leave her at my side? No, you can't take her! I wanted to run after her. All I was able to do was keep my uncontrollable sobs at bay. I am sorry, my baby.

The attendants said I would hurt my eyesight if I didn't stop crying, but the tears just kept rolling down my face. I stayed at Ae Ran Won for another month and then returned home. Before I left, all the girls sang a church hymn called "Until We Meet Again." The tune and voices in my head have survived all these years. At home, no one seemed to welcome me at all. Two other girls from Ae Ran Won followed me. They were my age, and we were like soul mates while we were there. They had nowhere else to go. But they had to leave, as nobody seemed to welcome them either. I looked long at their backs as they were leaving our home. Where would they go?

I was married six months later through a matchmaker. Friends and family kept telling me that the best way to forget all about my past was to marry and have children of my own. I bought their story, but everything wasn't the way they predicted. I adopted a child after ten years of trying to conceive one. Oh, what a brutal fate I had been dealt! I had to send away my own blood daughter. I am raising an adoptive child in her stead. I learned that the *jung* that would develop through being a parent to an adoptee is as great as that of a birth mother's. I love my adopted daughter as if my birth daughter was reincarnated and living within her. My child is now thirteen years old and she has one more year to finish her grade school. I am happy in my own way, and I thank Ae Ran Won and God.

My dear beloved daughter,

You were born in Korea, where we have four distinct seasons. It was September 23, 1984. The day was like a doorway to autumn, a time of the year when nothing like hot or cold exists. It was 7:05, to be exact, on a Sunday morning. God must have blessed your birth. We were comfortably tucked on the ondol floor side by side. You were crying as if you had to protest our short time together and our imminent farewell.

I touched your cheek and spoke to you in a soft, lulling voice. My baby, don't cry. God will bring you to your new adoptive parents, who are good and loving. You are born to the world through my body, but you will bloom under the loving care of your new parents. I, your mother, have led a life of the unfortunate, but I am placing you in a happy home. I believe God is gracious. Your happiness will be twice as much as the pain and unhappiness I have lived in. This confidence makes me happy.

There is no single day I forgot about you. I worried that you would be born sad because of my miserable life. I was shaken and weak during the pregnancy, too. I would pray to God that you would imitate God's loving character, so that you are loved and you would grow to be the evangelist of that love.

My baby! You would now be twenty years old and I am hoping you have become a beautiful woman. I just remember you as a baby, but you were just like me, big eyes and very rosy lips. My blood type is O, and I wonder what type yours is. My type is known to possess a very bright character. But my beloved daughter! God will look inside you rather than at your outward appearance. You are loved more when you possess a good heart. I'd like you to be a good daughter and show gratitude to your adoptive parents. I gave you a name when you were born. I called you Yuri. I wanted you to live a shiny and transparent life like glass. Your name sounds so pretty to the ears and easy to say. I pray to God you are filled with His blessings.

My alter ego and my daughter! I can't quite look at you with my own eyes, but you are always with me and will be always. You are my other life. Thus, you are everything to me. You were born to be loved, not to be abandoned. Your grandmother and your aunts are always praying for you. Everyone, including God, loves you so much. You should be grateful for the love and the grace. I believe God will guide you and will not spurn you. Study hard and become someone willing to help others in need. Be in good health and be joyous.

My beloved daughter, I love you so much. Bye, and let's not cry when we happen to meet in the future. Let's hold each other like two friends coming back from a short trip. Be healthy and respect yourself. Good-bye, my baby.

Korea has been a male-dominated society due to the influence by Confucianism. Women were considered to be the property of men. According to this worldview, a woman's chasteness was regarded as indispensable if she were to be married. Even if a woman was sexually harassed by a man, her best choice was to marry him; that was the only available option for her to gain the acceptance of the community. If she didn't marry him, whether by choice or circumstance, she was scorned by her neighbors and blamed even by her family members. People treated her as a filthy woman. If she did marry, a woman had to devote herself to her husband, no matter how irrationally she was treated.

Hwa-Byung (translated as "anger syndrome"), a very complex mental disease due to depression, was derived from the lives of Korean women in these types of situations. It was classified as "Korean ethnic syndrome" and included in the diagnostic manual *DSM-4* by the American Psychiatric Association in 1995. It was common among Korean women in those days.

Of course, times have changed, and the traditional point of view about male-female relations is not as dominant. However, the unequal treatment of and discrimination against women still remain, as well as the prejudice toward unwed single mothers.

The woman in this story also accepted her situation as her fate and took her only option, which was to marry the man who had raped her. Readers from the other side of the world might find it hard to understand her choice. Any Korean woman, however, would understand what she had been through and why she made the choice she did.

$\mathcal{L}$et's Meet for Sure

(baby born in 1990)

Today is June 1, 2006.

Minki, my first child God allowed me to have. It's your seventeenth birthday. I know you're only sixteen in American age, but I insist that it's your seventeenth. How can I forget the one year that you were inside of me?

There is a diary that I put in a drawer and pull out to read every time I miss you. Today also, I pulled it out and read it.

> *May 29, 1990.*
> What is life, and what does it mean? The theory that is not experienced is useless. Never useful. Why did God grant pain I can't cope with? I will be mature. My body and also my mind. I'll forgive. I definitely will.

June 2, 1990.
May 9 in lunar calendar (June 1 in solar calendar)
8:30 evening, eight pounds four ounces, a boy. He
looked like his dad. He was healthy. I hope God
forgives me.

June 7, 1990.
It was a hot day; it looked like it was going to rain.
I decided to give up my child for adoption. I want
to get counseling one more time. Which is the
right decision? I really don't know. However, I
want to take responsibility.

June 8, 1990.
I am full of a sense of betrayal. Why did I commit
this outrageous crime? Forgive me, God, and console me. Whenever I think about Minki, there's
nothing to do but shed tears.

The years passed so fast I didn't notice how I spent the
time. God showed me and shepherded me to the way.

My son, Minki! I was born in Daegu, in the north
Kyounsang province, Korea, in 1969. My grandmother was
alive. I have parents, three younger sisters, and a younger
brother. It was a big family. I think I resemble my parents
half and half. I was five foot one, a tall girl who had big
double-lidded eyes and a round face. I remember that my
grandma especially liked me. My father did also. I
remember that he picked me up and put me on his
shoulders. I remember that he smiled at me.

However, those are about good memories. My childhood memory is fragmented, in pieces. Later, I noticed that I put my bad memories into my subconscious. I found out that I was almost domestically adopted when I was about three. My mother had a really hard time because of my father, who had no money and liked to drink. She disappeared, abandoning me and my sister. After my aunt found out, she took us to an orphanage in Daegu. I was adopted by a family through the orphanage, and my sister was also about to be adopted, by another family. When my mom heard the news she ran back home. She begged my father's pardon, told her circumstances to the orphanage center, and made sure that they knew she would take care of us well. She stopped the adoptions and took us back home.

The memories of my life with my parents that I remembered after I grew up are of terribly hard times. My parents separated after my mother ran away from home three times. I remember that I had to hide with my sister and brother every night because of my father's violent behavior and drinking, his hunger and ignorance and anger. I hated my father, who hit us, but I couldn't forgive my mother even more because she ran away and abandoned us. I had to take care of my four younger siblings and do all the housework after she ran away. The hard times continued, and my father still scared me. He made me clean his uniform after he came home from work, and asked me to dry and iron it the next morning. I was in junior high at the time, but I had to do the laundry, dry it with a towel all night, hang it on the wall and iron it the next morning, because we had no washing machine. I couldn't get enough sleep.

When I was a freshman in high school, I had to quit school and work by helping at my father's store because of my family's bad financial situation. I met your dad around that time. Your daddy was a university student and his parents were alive. He was the first son and he had a younger sister, who was one year younger than him, and a younger brother, also one year younger. He was tall, had big eyes, and wore glasses. He was quiet and listened to me well. I met him when he was a customer at my workplace. I used to go to his house and I met his family. His sister was quite a pretty woman; she participated in a beauty contest. We were together for about two years.

As far as I can see now, I didn't love your dad. How could I know love as a person who didn't ever receive love? I was happy at that time just because I had someone who listened to me. Moreover, he studied a lot and was a decent person who grew up in a peaceful family. I wanted to be his friend. I was happy simply to be with him. He valued me very much. I think I was happy and laughed a lot at that time.

Minki, you were conceived in that happiness. I felt happiness for the first time while I was with him. However, I was very confused when I found that I was pregnant. We were selfish people who only thought about our pleasure. We didn't recognize what it would mean to have you in our lives.

I realized that I was pregnant in the fourth month, and I told your dad. Your dad's reaction made no sense and made me even more frustrated. He broke my heart by insisting that the baby was not his. He wouldn't even recognize you as a living being. He insisted that I had to abort you, and he wouldn't meet me because I didn't listen to him. I couldn't tell the truth to my father, who scared me. So I asked for help from my mother, who only kept in contact with me occasionally on the phone. She was surprised, and asked me who the father was, then persuaded me that we should meet him together. But he had taken his stand, and wanted to force me to go with his sister to have an abortion. After my mother realized that he had turned his back on me and that he was not a capable person who could take responsibility for me, she also wanted me to have an abortion and to start a new life. So your father contacted my mother when I was in my eighth month and together they tried to force me to be operated on for an abortion.

I don't know whether his parents knew this or not, but his sister knew. She took me to the hospital, persuaded me to have a stillbirth, and talked to the doctor. Your dad had changed into a totally different person compared to earlier, when he made me happy. Why did he behave like this? Was he scared? Was he also scared like me? Is that why he changed like that? I couldn't understand it. Here was a life that would be a beautiful baby in a month. How could I kill it? I was full of rejection.

The doctor tried to calm me by rationalizing the abortion, but I wanted to escape right away. Everything was scary. They took me to the operating table, prepared for the operation, and injected me with an anesthetic. But I threw up from the feeling of his rejection and betrayal, and they couldn't continue with the operation. I screamed at your dad and my mother not to force me to do this. Never again. I finally realized the fact that the only person who could take responsibility for you was me, myself. I didn't want to show myself to my siblings, so I couldn't go to my father's house. So I entered Ae Ran Won instead, after a neighbor told me about it.

I was staying at Ae Ran Won, but I was full of a sense of betrayal and anger at your father. I wanted to get revenge. I thought about giving birth to the baby and carrying it to his school, then showing the baby to him while everyone was watching. I thought I might give him the same pain that I had.

At that time, I didn't even know that there was a place to support people like me. From life in Ae Ran Won, and from the fact that we were all in a similar situation, I received a lot of consolation. I could see the situation objectively, little by little, and I could think seriously about what was the best for my baby. Even though I might ruin his life as I progressed with my plan, what is the use of it, if it causes unhappiness for all of us? I thought seriously about the meaning of parenthood. My thoughts about you changed several times in a day, and I understood the role of parents. If only you could be happy, I thought, I would give everything, even my life.

I sometimes imagine how we would be now. What if I didn't send you for adoption and we lived together? At that time, everyone—including my mother—who talked to me said I should send you for adoption not only for you, but also for myself. But I wanted to live with you. I had a huge guilty conscience. That is because I had always blamed my mother, because she left us and ran away from home, but I was committing a more serious sin. I hated to admit that. I sometimes found that I, like an idiot, was waiting for your dad to come back to me.

I painfully decided to send you for overseas adoption. Ae Ran Won connected me with an adoption agency, and one day I sat face to face with a social worker from there. She asked me about my choices, either the United States or Europe, and whether I would prefer adoptive parents who have a particular religion. I chose the United States, and a Christian family. That was the only thing I could do for you. I chose the United States, where there are many opportunities, because of my painful experiences. I didn't want you to have to repeat my sad memories in this poor country, like when I couldn't make breakfast in the morning because there was no rice anymore, or I couldn't go to school because I had no transportation fee.

Minki! I can't forget the short night I spent with you. The pain of giving birth for the first time was unbearable. I couldn't say it's painful while I was in labor, that an unmarried woman giving birth without a husband in Korea was a very shameful thing at that time, so I didn't want to bring attention to myself. I was ashamed. I felt so sad when I was giving birth to you in the maternity hospital with the help of a midwife, thinking that I had to send my baby away. You were born crying, after thirteen long hours of labor. That dark night, the time I spent with you was so precious to me because I knew that the people from the adoption agency would be coming to take you in the morning. I was so thankful that I gave birth to you at night, so I could have more time with you. I tried to give you one more hug even though I was so tired and sleepy after the birth. I wanted to give you as much body heat as I could. I wanted to give you my love also. I hated myself so much when I went back to Ae Ran Won to get postpartum care, after the adoption people came to take you early in the morning. My thoughts about you were even more sincere after I gave birth to you than when you were inside me. I just cried. I just kept crying.

Minki! I tried to be indifferent when a social worker from the adoption agency came to me and let me know they gave you your name, Minki. I tried to think "What does it matter after I gave them charge of your future?" and I tried hard to forget. I only prayed. I prayed every day for God to take care of you. That was the only thing I could do for you.

After giving birth, there were a lot of changes in me. Through counseling, I decided to keep studying, which I had stopped. I started studying again and passed the qualification test for high school graduation. I wanted to go to college, too, and Ae Ran Won offered a scholarship if I did. However, I had four younger siblings. I gave up entering the university and chose to get a job because I had to support their studies. I was so happy because, fortunately, I was able to join a comparatively big company and it was a nice job. I was proud to get a job with only a high school diploma! I was so pleased. I slowly got peace of mind with a plan for the future, when I would become financially stable.

Around that time, a letter and some pictures from your adoptive parents gave me comfort. They seemed like nice parents. You looked like a cute and beloved son. I still keep those precious pictures. I pull out the pictures whenever I miss you. I was so happy because you are growing up healthy and your parents are with you.

I remember your first birthday after I sent you away. I spent all day thinking about you, imagining your face. How have your crying voice, big eyes, and round forehead changed? You may grow up recognizing people around you, but what if you are crying, looking for someone who looks like you among the people who look different from you? Are you ever sick? So many thoughts captured me. I trusted that your adoptive parents were taking good care of you, but sometimes I suddenly felt anxious. Whenever I felt like that, I ran to the adoption agency to get news about you.

After that, I visited the adoption agency several times, but I didn't hear anything anymore. So I had to leave my information with them and listen to "no news is good news" from the social workers there. They said, "There's no way to contact your child if he doesn't look for his birth mother after he becomes an adult." I had to stop walking in each time with tears of yearning and frustration.

However, I believed that God, who saved you, who let you be born in this world through me, and who gave you people to bring you up with love, will listen to my prayer for you.

After that, around the time I recovered from the hurt and felt comfort again, I was introduced by an acquaintance to someone I could marry. I confessed honestly about my experience and your existence to him. He left me after he heard my story. I expected that, but it was painful. However, how could I be happy denying your existence? That is because I am your mother. I thought I couldn't abandon you twice. I hope I can meet you openly when you come to me someday.

Time passed like that. The wound was hidden deep inside. There was a time when I could face myself, which I had to deal with by pretending there wasn't a wound. I finally looked for a cure. I could forgive my parents at that time. And I know how much God, whom I thought only severed himself from me, had been loving me, and had prepared an amazing plan for me.

●

Five years later, I met my husband. God gave me a thankful husband who knows love and loves me sincerely. How wonderful that someone has eyes and a heart that can read and see others sincerely?

He panicked a little and wavered when I told him that I had given birth to a son as an unwed single mother and sent him to the United States for adoption. But that was only for a moment. He accepted me because I told him the truth in spite of the fact that he could have left me. Then he told me that when he was in the middle of theological seminary, a professor asked the students a question. "If God gives you a woman like Gomer, would you obey Him as Hosea did?" (In the Bible, Gomer was a prostitute whom God commanded the prophet Hosea to marry.) Then the professor pointed especially at my future husband and asked the question once more. He was puzzled, but he answered that he would. After that, he answered "yes" with a heart of obedience. I was so full of appreciation that God prepared my husband for this.

This is the tenth year since we got married with the blessings of nice people. God blessed us and gave us four children. In the middle of changing their diapers, giving them milk, reading them a book, giving them baths, eating something delicious, watching their smiling faces, traveling somewhere, taking them to school, reprimanding them, or walking them, I am reminded of you. You have always remained in my heart.

I appreciate your parents. I hope you can understand what I am trying to say. People who know about love can bring up a child with love and honor, without treating the child as a possession. Sometimes it is not easy even to constantly love your own child. How great a love it would be to worry about a child, whether the child is sick or not, comfortable or not, hungry or not! If ever you and your adoptive parents would visit me, I really would like to say this to them: "Thank you."

Now I am as happy as can be. There are your four younger siblings whom I want to show you. One of them looks like you. You are probably curious and want to see them, aren't you? Even though your birth father is gone, I am so happy because I am with a wonderful husband who loves me and is waiting for you with me, and saying that he would willingly be your father. I am studying social work, which I wanted to do, as well as going through reading and essay teacher training. Because of my life, even though it is neither rich nor insufficient, and because God is with me, I am so happy.

Minki! I want to see you. I want to meet you. I go to Ae Ran Won every summer to meet the adoptees and their families coming from the United States.

Some of them are the same age as you. Whenever I meet them, I am curious about why you can't come even though they can, and I sometimes cry. As time goes by, I wait for you, and I hope more and more to meet you. Do you also miss me? Are you curious about what your birth mother is like? I am curious about whether we look like each other, what your hobbies are, what your dreams are, whether you have a religion, whether you also watch the Oprah Winfrey show (I only watch it because I heard that is a popular show in the United States, and might help me understand American culture. I want to reduce the cultural gap between you and me when we meet), what kind of Korean food you like to eat, who you respect, and whether you have a girlfriend.

My husband is a really wonderful person who writes me a letter on your birthday every year. He also sent me a congratulatory text message on your sixteenth birthday. I am going to send it to you also.

Minki! I love you so much. I love you regardless of what you are like. Don't be sick, be healthy. Let's meet for sure while we are alive.

From your birth mom, waiting for you.

 ### A note from Sangsoon Han

Her birth son turned 18 in 2008. She visited the adoption agency, and asked to search for her son. The agency was able to find the boy, and learned that he had just graduated from high school. The boy was so shocked that his birth mother was searching for him that he asked the agency to have the birth mother send him a letter and pictures, so that he would more fully believe that it was his birth mother. She wrote him a letter, and sent it along with a few pictures of her family. Now she is eagerly waiting for his reply.

$\mathscr{P}$lease Be Healthy and Happy

(baby born in 1994)

In 1994, I delivered a baby daughter and sent her to the
United States for adoption. Ever since then, I have been
longing for her to come back and find me. Whenever I
meet adoptees who are searching for their parents, I always
tell them that the reason they were given up for adoption
was because their mothers had really loved them and that,
at the time, it was the best solution for their happiness.
Each year, I attend Ae Ran Won's annual reunion so that I
can tell this to adoptees and I hope always to continue.
I always look forward to summertime when many adoptees
come to their homeland to search for their parents.

I, myself, was also adopted. My birth mother was a teacher
who gave birth to me when she was twenty years old and
unwed. Of course, she couldn't afford to raise me by herself,

and I don't even know who my father is. At first, I didn't know I was an adopted child. My adoptive parents couldn't have a baby so they adopted me and then they adopted a relative's son in order to continue the family line. I was treated unfairly after they adopted the relative's son. My adoptive parents liked him better than me. I didn't understand why at the time. One day, when I came home from school, my adoptive mother gave my brother a pear. Since pears are my favorite fruit, I asked her to give me one too but she said that there weren't any left. A few minutes later, I went into the kitchen and checked the cupboard. Sure enough, there were several pears in there. For many years, I was hurt and couldn't understand why she acted like that. Finally, in middle school, I understood the reason. It was because I was not their child. I found out from a friend who lived in the same village. I was then able to understand the relationship between my parents and me.

After finishing middle school I wanted to go on to high school, but my parents wouldn't let me, even though they could afford it. So I had to give up my dreams and just settle for becoming independent. One day, I got a job through my aunt. My workplace was far from home so I rented a room in a boarding house near there. I started on my own two feet. I worked very hard and was making a life for myself.

Then, a terrible thing happened to me. One night, when my landlord and his wife were out, their son raped me. After that, I didn't want to live there anymore and thought about killing myself. My landlord and his wife wanted me to marry their son. Other people wanted me to marry him too, so I thought I should. Although I knew he was a bad man with many problems, I thought that I had to marry him because he had raped me. I thought that since I had lost my virginity, I shouldn't marry another man so it was better to marry the man who raped me rather than kill myself.

After I had set the wedding date, my birth mother suddenly contacted me and wanted to see me. I was extremely uncomfortable because I was not ready to see her at the time. Later, I found out that her brother lived near me and that she had been checking up on me through him. She had heard that I was going to marry the landlord's son, who was not a reliable or responsible person, and that I would be unhappy if I married him. So she made up her mind to talk to me. However, I got really angry that she had known how difficult my circumstances were and hadn't helped me any earlier. I was just 18 years old and I hated my mother for giving me up and not being there when I needed her.

Eventually, I went to my uncle's house and met my birth mother for the first time. It was obvious that I wouldn't be happy if I married the landlord's son, so my birth mother urged me not to marry him. I did anyway, against her advice, and gave birth to my first daughter.

Hoping that my husband would change for our daughter, I tried as hard as I could to be patient with him. He had a mental problem, however, so he drank and hit me more with each passing day. My mother-in-law had passed away and we were living with my father-in-law. Since my husband was out of work, I began to make a living by setting up my own small restaurant. I even delivered milk at four in the morning before preparing breakfast for my family. Since I was working so much, I asked a neighbor to take care of the children while I did the shopping and worked at the restaurant until ten o'clock at night. Then I picked up my children and carried on with household duties until midnight.

My daily life didn't end there, though, because my husband would start verbally and physically abusing me. I was so tired mentally and physically that I couldn't take it anymore. I didn't know what to do about it and didn't think there was anything I could do. I got more and more depressed, cursing my fate. Meanwhile, my husband became more violent, punching, kicking, and even throwing things at me. I thought that if I had to endure any more, I would either go crazy or die, but I couldn't leave the house. I was five months pregnant.

Although my body and soul weakened under the threat of violence every night, I was the sole breadwinner in the family so I had to keep on working. All I could do was take medicines for my aches and pains. Eventually, though, I feared for my life and fled from home, leaving everything behind. I felt desperate, and couldn't ask anybody I knew for help, because then my husband might find out where I was. One day, I found Ae Ran Won through a social welfare agency. I felt no hesitation about going there, and at last I found some relief.

Nonetheless, I still had a very guilty conscience about leaving my children behind. I felt worthless and disgusted with myself. At that point, I really wanted to die. After receiving some counseling regarding my baby's future, I decided to give her up for overseas adoption. I thought it would be better for her because I had suffered all sorts of hardships as an adopted child in Korea. I thought America would be better than Korea, because Koreans have a prejudice toward adopted children. In my case, adoption would have been impossible because she was born to a married couple, so I said that the child wasn't my husband's.

I gave birth to my daughter on May 9, 1994. Owing to a severe pain in my heart, I had serious toxemia during childbirth and my blood pressure rose. Because of the danger, I had to have a cesarean section. After the baby was born, I felt intense anguish and couldn't bear to look at her because of my guilty conscience. I knew that I wouldn't be able to give up my baby if I saw her. I had no reason to live, and all I wanted was to die with my baby. One day, a social worker came to take her to the adoption agency. After they left, I was discharged from the hospital and returned to Ae Ran Won. It took a long time for my body to recover from childbirth. My anguish and the prolonged birthing pains probably hindered my recovery.

However, I slowly got better and became eager to see my baby. Even though I hadn't seen her yet, I was deeply, emotionally attached to her. I missed her badly. However, she had already been adopted, so I contacted the adoption agency to inquire about my baby and her adoptive parents.

At this stage, I was informed that my baby had a problem in the development of a part of her brain so her adoption was canceled the first time when the prospective family found out about it. Eventually, she was adopted again and underwent three operations. It was hard for me to bear all that had happened, and I lost my way again.

I was told by the social worker that my baby might lose the sense of sight. When I received a picture of my baby with a head tied up with white bandages, I blacked out. I wished for something that could take all my memories away. I don't remember how I made it back to Ae Ran Won. As soon as I saw the face of the social worker who was waiting for me in Ae Ran Won, I burst into tears. I was crying my heart out in her arms. I don't know how much time passed, but after a while I realized that the social worker was also crying, and I heard her crying even more loudly. I opened my eyes and looked at her and saw her crying as she really cares. I smiled. I was happy to know that someone else was crying for me. I was not by myself any more, I was not the only one left behind in the world. I stopped crying and could smile. I felt some dark clouds around me were clearing away and it seemed brighter than ever.

I found genuine warmth and affection in the social worker. She showed me that escaping from reality was not the way to solve problems. There, I found another world instead of the torturous reality I had faced. I stopped thinking about killing myself and started to see other possibilities. My will to live grew stronger, as well as my faith in God and my confidence in people to help me. I enrolled in a training program to become a cook. Through this process, I found hope again.

Years later, my heart still leaps and I am overcome with emotions when I remember my time at Ae Ran Won. I sometimes wonder what would have happened to me if I hadn't gone there. I might have had to wander the streets with no choice but to go back to my house and bear the baby alone. Also, in discovering my baby's handicap, I can only imagine what would have happened had my rage exploded. However, Ae Ran Won helped me and my family find a second chance in life. I had come with nothing but the clothes on my back and they offered me food, shelter, and clothing. They gave me a new perspective on life through counseling. After getting my license to be a cook, and while preparing to get my driver's license, I heard that my husband had become a Christian and was a changed man. I agonized about going back to him and came to understand that my family was in big trouble, especially my daughter, who was in her second year in high school and having to take care of her little brother after school as well as keeping the household. Ultimately, I decided to return home for my children.

Even though my husband promised not to be violent, he failed, and I had to go to a shelter for abused women with my son. Because I had been raised as an adopted child, I wanted to bring my children up myself despite my difficult circumstances. Earlier, I had been bitter toward my birth mother for abandoning me. After meeting her unexpectedly, I never wanted to see her again. However, through my own experiences, I was able to understand that she had probably been in great pain after giving me up. I then decided to contact my mother. I asked around and found out where she lived. I tried to meet her again, with my uncle's help, but she didn't want to see me anymore. I knew it was because she was afraid and not because she didn't care about me. I also knew from my own experience that she probably felt worthless as a mother and suffered from great guilt. In spite of her fear, she had reached out to me at first because of her concern over my marriage. Without counseling, I knew that I would have suffered the same remorse that she felt.

Despite my repeated attempts to make contact, she still refused to see me. Then I got into a near fatal traffic accident and was afraid that I would never have the chance to help my mother be rid of her sorrow. To my uncle, I threatened to kill myself if my mother did not agree to see me. My tactic worked and she finally relented. When I saw her face for the second time, I could see that it was full of trouble and that she had suffered greatly. I could recognize that she had led a life full of tears and regrets. I saw her two more times after that. I told her that I understood and forgave her. In our subsequent meetings, my mother lost her fear of me and her face looked peaceful. That made me feel light of heart, and we talked not as mother to daughter but as woman to woman about our shared experiences. I wished for my mother to live in peace for her remaining years.

In the future, when my mother feels comfortable enough to tell me about my father, I would like to learn about him. All I know is that he is not a good person. Nonetheless,

I would like to meet with him when the time is right and show him that I am a strong, solid person who overcame great obstacles. I also want the peace of mind that comes from forgiving him for the hardships that he has caused me and my mother. I wish him a comfortable life as well.

After the meetings with my mother, I visited the adoption agency several times for news about my daughter. A few days ago, I received a letter with a picture of a beautiful child. In the photo she is smiling brightly, and I felt certain that she was happy in her adoptive family, which eased my anxiety and grief. When I had the opportunity to go to America, I tried contacting as many adoption agencies as possible to locate my daughter and see her. The adoptive parents refused the visit, however, because they were afraid of the impact it would have on my daughter. The adoption agency said that when my daughter becomes an adult, she would be able to meet me if she wanted. So I am counting the days until we reunite. In the past, I wished for my life to end but now, I want to live for as long as possible in order to give my daughter time to grow up and decide to find me. In my case, it took a very long time for me to want to see my birth mother. I wish for my daughter to keep the words of Deuteronomy 6:5 in her mind. "And thou shalt love the Lord thy God with all thy heart, and with all thy soul, and with all thy might." Since she was born with special love, I want her to know the truth that God always loves her.

My dear daughter, I hope that you love Jesus and that you bring joy to everyone who knows you. I pray for you every day, and pray that we can meet someday. Until that day, please be healthy and happy. Every June and July, adoptive parents and adoptees from abroad visit Korea and meet with current and former residents of Ae Ran Won. It is a precious opportunity for them to talk and get to know one another. On one occasion, I had the chance to go to Minnesota to attend a celebration for adopted Korean children. While visiting the United States I attended meetings, observed a training program for adoptive parents, and visited a facility for unwed mothers. I was also impressed and touched by a family that had adopted only disabled children. Through these experiences, I decided to devote myself to helping adoptive parents, adoptees, and unwed mothers for the rest of my life.

One day, I happened to have a car accident and was close to death. At that time, I thought that I might never be able to see my youngest daughter again, so I instructed my oldest daughter to meet with her if anything should happen to me. However, I worried that I would be unable to answer any questions that she might have, such as why I had to give her up, so I am quite happy and relieved to be alive and able to record these words. I appreciate my baby's adoptive parents for raising her to be beautiful and healthy in spite of her three operations. Thank you.

After returning home, this woman has been making great efforts to create a family with her husband. Her son had been emotionally damaged and suffered from an attachment disorder resulting from neglect, so, for three years, they had to apply for financial aid and medical services from a social medical fund to treat him. Through the tremendous care she gave her son, he slowly recovered and is now completely healed. She still has difficulties in her relationship with her husband, as it has not been easy for him to change all at once. But he is gradually making progress through his faith in God.

She, on the other hand, has changed completely. Now, she realizes her own importance and makes time and effort for her physical and spiritual health. She actively tries to solve her problems rather than avoid or internalize them. Nowadays, instead of meeting with violence, she has managed to stand up for herself and hold her husband accountable for his actions. She not only lets him know when he has done wrong, but encourages him to correct his mistakes. Although there will continue to be many difficult moments in the future, she is empowered to live a different life from the past for herself and her two children. She is also preparing her husband and children for the day they meet her birth daughter. She meets with adoptees from abroad and from Korean families and explains why their mothers could not keep them. In doing so, she hopes to lessen the adoptees' emotional burdens.

chapter 4

$\mathscr{A}$ Solid Foundation

(baby born in 1995)

To my lovely and precious baby,

This is to help those who were adopted overseas, like my child, in understanding the social and cultural background of Korea, their motherland. I was born into a family of four: parents, an elder brother, and myself. My parents raised livestock for a living. They were somewhat partial to my brother because of Confucian practice in Korea which dictates that only sons can perform the family rituals for ancestor worship. I was mistreated and physically abused for being a daughter. I was a physically weak child. However, I tried to study hard to win attention and affection from my parents. I even went so far as to read a book while walking along the road. Through my efforts, I was awarded a prize by the Ministry of Science and Technology for outstanding achievement.

All my aspirations were shattered by my brother, however, who abused me continually. I could not tell my parents because they loved him dearly and treated him like a prince in the family. My parents finally found out the truth and to my surprise, my brother was not blamed. In my heart, I felt anger and hatred settling in. I was ranked the number one or two student in my class, but soon dropped to last place. I realized that there were certain things that I could not change. All I had was despair, even after doing the best I could to improve my life.

I barely graduated from high school and got a job. At first, I only took care of some coupons. Later, I was appointed team leader, supervising female employees in the company. My family was becoming financially stable but, unfortunately, my father started having affairs with other women. My parents got into quarrels frequently and my father physically abused my mother. In the end he got sick, so I quit the company where I worked for four years to take care of my father. I had no choice, and I was resentful about my bad luck. I longed and longed for a better life and even though I did the best I could, it was still the same agonizing life . . . until I met the father of my baby. He was younger than my brother, and instantly we formed a connection. We became very good friends. He was caring and warm to me when I had so much pain in my heart. I was very afraid of intimacy with a man but he restored my trust. I hated staying at home, so I naturally spent more time with him at his place. But his parents opposed our relationship because of the social gap between us. I did not know this at the beginning, but he was from a well-to-do family; his father was a doctor and his mother was a teacher.

Later on, I realized that I was pregnant. When I heard this news, I was very surprised and worried but, on the other hand, I was very happy to have a child with the man I loved. His reaction, though, was quite different from what I expected. He actually insisted on abortion, saying that he was a student with no financial independence. I could not agree to this because the baby was ours and the result of our love. My solution was to die together with the baby. I'm not sure whether I was lucky or not, but he found me and sent me to a hospital to have my stomach pumped, and I survived the attempt to die. In the end, his parents decided to send him to the United States and I was left alone in Korea. I didn't know what to think, and I felt so lonely. To be an unwed mother in Korea is like being branded with a scarlet letter on one's chest. It is considered a family shame as well. Women in that condition are treated very badly in society as it is unacceptable in Korean culture.

However, I wanted to save my baby's life at any cost. So, I left my house and rented a small room to start a new life with my baby. Luckily, my friends helped me get through this. For the first three months, I managed to get by but as my belly grew bigger and bigger, my neighbors looked at me with questions and curiosity. In order to keep me safe, one of my friends, who was also a friend of my baby's father, had the idea to tell the neighbors that he was the father and had to live in another town because of his job. This worked fine, and I was accepted and free from prejudice. Being pregnant was made more difficult because I could not do anything to make a living. As time went on, my worries grew bigger because I was running out of money.

My friend contacted my mother back home and we met. At that time, it was near the due date. As soon as my mother saw me, she started crying. I could not talk much and she kept asking what I would do with the baby. I knew I could not support my baby the way others could, by providing a good education or even decent food. I could not bear the pain of seeing my baby mistreated by others because she has an unwed mother and no father. There was nothing I could do for this precious one. For days, I sought a solution and finally decided to go to Ae Ran Won and think about putting my baby up for adoption.

There, I met many mothers in the same situation and I felt much safer and more comfortable. The counseling was great and helpful. I thought about my baby's future and wanted my baby to have a chance in another country rather than being in Korea under poverty and social disdain. I knew that living in Korea as a girl was tough and I did not want her to inherit that discrimination. I wanted my baby to have better conditions in life than I had. I thought it over and over and always came to the same conclusion: to send her overseas for adoption. If I was selfish, I could have kept her with me and raised her in Korea. My decision for overseas adoption was made so she could grow up in a better environment, free from prejudice and discrimination.

From Ae Ran Won, I learned that open adoption was available when doing an overseas adoption. They also told me that my child could have opportunities to meet and be supported by other adoptees.

At that time, there were some programs going on at Ae Ran Won for adopting families visiting Korea. Through one of these programs, I had a chance to meet and talk with overseas adoptees and their families. I could feel true love and connection between them. Somehow, despite the inevitable pain of separation, I knew that my decision for overseas adoption was the right thing to do.

Before delivery, I was scared and nervous. However, after having my baby next to me, I experienced true pain in my heart. With my child in my arms, I thought about having to separate from her the next morning. I could not sleep that night. All I could think of was running away with my baby in my arms. I hated not being able to carry out my desire. If there had been a system to support rather than blame unwed mothers in Korea, I could still have my baby with me. Under current circumstances, though, what else could I do? I had to think about my baby's future. She would have experienced poverty and hunger if I had kept her, because I didn't have the means to take care of her needs.

I thought about the kind of adoptive parents I wanted for my child. I wanted my baby to experience lots of love with her adoptive parents. I wanted the kind of couple who were unable to have their own child so they could dearly love and care for my child and raise her to be healthy and sound.

Luckily, my child has fine parents. I met them in person when they were in Korea to pick her up and take her to the United States. I held their hands tightly and cried for a long time. Meeting them in person helped me to be sure that I was doing the right thing for the baby. Just like that, I sent my child away to another country.

Having an open adoption made it possible to exchange some letters and presents with her on her birthday every year. If the day should come for us to meet in the future, I want to tell her why I had to give her up. Some people accused me of abandoning my child. But I never ever gave up on my child. I just wanted to provide a better environment for her to grow up in and have more chances in life. I want my child to have a better life than mine. I want her to be able to achieve whatever she wants in life. Every night, I pray for her happiness and her new family in the United States.

After being separated from my daughter, I started to develop myself. I promised myself not to get stuck on feeling sad. Ae Ran Won has some vocational programs and I signed up for computer training. I knew that the program would give me an opportunity to be financially independent, so I did my best. Finally, I got a job in a computer-related field after completing the program in six months. Since the adoption was an open adoption, my child would know where I live. Some day, she could come and meet me. I wanted to be able to show her that I tried hard to live with pride and strength. At the time of our reunion, I would like to be a proud mother, rather than an ashamed one.

Now, all I want is to create a solid foundation for the future. I know it requires that I work harder than others to achieve it. For the sake of my child, I want to earn enough money to support her if she ever needs my help in the future. For that reason, I save a part of my salary for her in a savings account. I am taking steps to make my dream come true.

With my life a little more settled, I worked hard and saved some money. I married a man who knew my story and had loved me for a long time. It was comforting not having to hide my past, so I decided to marry him. I had two boys with him, but the marriage was not that easy to maintain. He did not directly express his feelings about my past during our marriage, but I learned that he couldn't deal with it. He started having affairs and then physically abused me. Out of despair, I got divorced and he took my two boys and my money. Due to the stress and shock, my boys were in and out of the hospital. My ex-husband could not handle this situation, and in the end I took the boys back.

For three years, we suffered a series of hardships. I had to take care of two young children and also work outside the home to survive. The three of us went through a tough time. It was unbearable at times to continue, but I thought of my first child overseas and regained some strength that helped me work to improve the situation for my other two children. I wanted to raise them well, so I did not take serious work. I figured that later on I could have financial stability.

My first child could come to see me at any time, so I
wanted to be ready for her and show her how proud her
mother is in Korea. I went through a lot of prejudice after
revealing my past as an unwed mother. It is too much for
unwed mothers to deal with. Although new husbands show
willingness to understand our situation, it doesn't seem that
easy for them to take in. And even though open adoption
offers more advantages than closed adoption, many unwed
mothers still hesitate to go for it. The prejudice prevents the
mothers from coming forward to meet the adopted child
when they come to Korea to search for them. It would
greatly disrupt their current lives. Korean culture is very
different from that of the United States and Europe.

After all these years, I finally got to meet my daughter.
The adoptive parents have two other adopted Korean
children and my daughter was their third child. When she
turned ten, the family brought her to Korea to meet me.
I have a small apartment to take my child in during her stay
in Korea. Hearing the news that they were coming to
Korea, I bought a secondhand car to take them around. As I
always wanted, I was able to offer them my apartment to
stay in and take them around Korea in my own car. In that
way, I made my dreams come true. My daughter has grown
up healthy and I could meet the parents who nurtured my
child so well. I was just happy.

Looking at my daughter, I would have gone through all
those tough times all over again. I felt right about my
decision to send her away for adoption. I am so thankful to
my daughter's adoptive mother for all her efforts to raise

my child to be as beautiful as she is now. Our karma was so special. For me, all the siblings of my daughter are like my children and I feel so much appreciation to her adoptive sister and brother and got to see what a happy child she is. She has two mothers: one in Korea and the other in the States. Both of them love and adore her, so it's no wonder she is so lucky and happy! By reading this story, it is my humble wish for adoptees to understand where the mothers come from and why they needed to send their children to other countries for adoption. I hope that reading this helped you to understand. Thank you for reading.

 A note from Sangsoon Han

In the time since writing this story, the birth mother learned that the adoptive parents got divorced. She was shocked to hear the news. Subsequently, the birth mother herself got divorced from her husband, and she came to understand more about the problems involved. She also saw that the adoptive parents continued to communicate and raise their child, even though they were divorced, and she was happy to see that. She and the adoptive mother remain in close communication.

chapter 5

$\mathcal{Y}$ou Were Born to be Loved

(baby born in 1996)

I hope Korean adoptees will be able to understand and forgive their birth mothers through my story. Maybe I am hoping too much, but I still hope my story can comfort you even a little. This is why I decided to tell you about my past, which has been difficult to tell.

It was a small, peaceful, and beautiful city in America.
A blue lake filled my eyes with hope and I was at peace as I watched ducks floating serenely.

With a different language and appearance, I didn't have any friends to talk to. All I could do was just sit there alone and look at the lake every afternoon. Why did I have to go all the way there? Why did I have to bear this difficult loneliness? Why did I have to decide to take this risk?

As if having noticed my confusion, the sunshine gently caressed me. The loneliness in an unfamiliar city, fears of an uncertain future, and the past trauma . . . all these I endured because I had something precious to keep, even though that meant giving up everything else. I had to keep the life of the baby growing inside me.

I don't want to avoid my painful past because that includes the beginning of ties with my baby.

●

My story goes back to a spring day in my hopeful early twenties, when I met a guy who changed my whole life. When I was working after I graduated from the university, one of my colleagues set us up. He was ten years older than me and was an artist with diverse experiences and a unique personality. I wasn't attracted to him right away, but I began to like him after a few dates. As a good adviser in my life, he started to mean something to me. He said that he liked my clean pure soul and I fell in love with him. We truly loved each other for a while and began to think about marriage. But unfortunately our love didn't last very long.

As time went by, he became demanding. I was young and naive with little experience of the world. He wanted me to be a grown up woman with a refined attitude and intelligence. I was thankful for his advice and thought I had to change myself in the way he wanted me to. However, I couldn't change myself as much as I wanted, which made me feel worthless and miserable. I was disappointed that he didn't love me the way I was, but at the same time I blamed myself for not being good enough for him. I found myself trying to obey him just because I loved him, which was foolish.

One day he asked me to break up. The reason was that I couldn't live up to his expectations. I could neither understand nor accept it because I felt the reason he gave me was trivial. It was a great shock to me. I did everything to get him back. I begged him to come back, swallowing my pride. In actuality, though, his mind had already walked away from me, and there was nothing left that I could do.

After that, I suffered from a sense of loss and hurt. However, I didn't have much time to be sad. Soon after the breakup, I discovered that I was pregnant. I felt desperate and lost. Since I couldn't handle the situation, I asked one of my close friends for help. As a thoughtful friend and a devout Christian, she understood my situation and tried to comfort me. She helped me see an obstetrician, and made me think twice about abortion. After much thinking, I decided to tell my ex-boyfriend about the pregnancy. However, after being told everything, he suggested I get an abortion, as if it was the only thing to do.

He told me that he was an adoptee. He somehow found out, and learned it was true when he was in junior high. Since then he has been lonely and unhappy, feeling as if he was a plant without roots. He made an earnest request for abortion, saying that he didn't want his child to go through what he had been through. Realizing he wouldn't be able to change my mind, he warned me that he was going to tell my parents everything.

He was stubborn enough to say that if my parents knew about this, they would do everything to stop me from having the baby. I didn't expect him to marry me after he was told about the baby, but his cold attitude broke my heart. If my parents found out about my pregnancy, it was obvious that they would be shocked and force me to have an abortion. My mom would suffer even more, since my conservative father would definitely blame her for not fulfilling her responsibility to educate me properly. I could imagine him criticizing her for humiliating our family.

To be an unwed single mother in Korea means being isolated from your family, friends, and acquaintances. I probably would have to cut off all connections and go to a place where no one knew me. Since the secret could not be kept forever, people would soon discover that I was an unwed single mother. I thought I deserved all the blame, but that I could do everything for my baby even though I wasn't financially independent. However, I couldn't let my baby be blamed and hurt because of me. This led me to decide to have an abortion. It seemed like the only solution.

A priest I met changed my mind. After his counseling, I realized that the life of my baby was from God, and that abortion is murder. The priest made it clear that although I had sinned against God, he was hoping I would save my baby. I saw my own ugliness as I was about to take a life.

I became aware of the grace of God, who was giving me hope to live.

With a belief in God, I made up my mind to save my baby. Nothing had changed, but I found peace. It was a gift from God. I left for America with the help of the priest and one of my friends. I lied to my boyfriend and told him that I had had an abortion. My parents thought I was going to take a language course in America. The priest arranged for me to stay in an American home. At that time, I was three months pregnant.

It was a small pretty house beside a beautiful lake. The host couple was busy but very nice to me. I was usually left alone after breakfast. I sat by the lake and spent time talking to my baby, reading books, or listening to music. I also looked back on my life. The time in Korea had been filled with pain, but my life in America, where I couldn't communicate, was extremely lonely. But it wasn't totally bad, because I was with my baby. When I returned to Korea to give birth, I had to face another life.

Right after my return to Korea, I was accepted into Ae Ran Won, a place for unmarried mothers. At Ae Ran Won, I met many other unmarried mothers with their own stories. It was a shock to meet young unmarried mothers who had been through worse things than me. However, it was not easy to live with others. My self-esteem went down when I had to admit my status as an unmarried mother. Still, we had things in common. We all had the fear of giving birth and we all had to let our babies go.

The things we shared made us aware of the fact that we were all mothers. This led us to understand and help one another. The devout love of the people at Ae Ran Won also supported me a lot.

I still remember the Christmas I spent there. We decided to hold a party and perform a play. As we prepared for the play, we became one with each other. Each of us talked about our stories: why we were there, how we were feeling, and our plans after sending the babies away. Through the play, we were able to see ourselves in an objective way. We cried and laughed together. We were happy because we understood one another.

Among other things, several programs at Ae Ran Won helped me a lot. Group counseling about how to decide the baby's future was especially useful. My baby and I were lucky to be able to get a lot of information on adoption. Vague concerns about the future of my baby turned to hope.

Before becoming an unmarried mother, I thought adoption was only for abandoned babies. However, after being told about many adoption cases, I realized it could be another beautiful choice for birth mothers and adoptive parents, because they loved their babies.

Ae Ran Won provided classes and counseling about the adoption system. I compared domestic adoption with foreign adoption, which helped me make the right choice for me. I chose an open foreign adoption so that I would be able to keep in touch with my baby. Domestic adoption also had considerable merits. However, one of the most important things I considered was whether I would be able to hear from my baby. I wanted know who the adoptive parents would be and check on the status of my baby to make sure he would be happy and safe. I also wanted my baby to know about me. I thought my baby would like to know why he had to be adopted. For a healthy adoption, I thought it would be necessary to share the facts and together fight through whatever difficulties we would face.

Children's Home Society of Minnesota (CHSM) in America was well aware of this and had a good education program. I thought a foreign adoption through CHSM would be the best choice. It would be another scar for both my baby and me if I were not able to hear from him or meet him for the rest of my life. Although it was shameful, I wanted to tell my baby who I am, and see how my baby would grow up with good adoptive parents. It would probably be a dangerous decision to reveal who I am; however, it was the only option I could take for my lovely baby.

On December 29, 1996, a cold, wintry day, I gave birth to a boy after severe suffering. After having spent a night together, I had to send him to an adoption agency without a decent hug because I was so tired after his birth. This painful memory still hurts me. My sorrow was heavy as the new year came without him. The only thing left to do was to find good adoptive parents for him. I think I was extremely lucky because I had the chance to meet his adoptive parents in advance. I was invited to a program for potential adoptive parents in Minnesota organized by

CHSM. My boy's adoptive parents looked very excited and showed me a picture of the baby's room. Since they were very nice people, I felt relieved.

After he was adopted, I had the chance to meet him while staying in America for a language course. Ever since then, I have been receiving pictures, videotapes, and letters once a year from his adoptive parents. I have also been sending him a birthday card and a small gift every year, and keeping in touch with them by email. Two years ago, I was again invited to the same program in Minnesota and able to meet my boy and his adoptive parents. It took great courage to actually meet him, but facing my painful past allowed me the chance to move on. The fact that he was growing up so well encouraged me to go on with my life. It was not just pain, but it was hope at the same time. Although I cannot live with my boy, I always see him from a distance and try to do my best not to be a shameful mother.

I wrote my story hoping it would comfort Korean adoptees. Looking back, everything seems like a miracle and I am thankful.

I believe my baby is a great gift and blessing from God. Through having him, I realized how precious life is. I had the courage to continue with my life, and most of all I realized the love of God. I now have a more profound view of my life, and I found how to deal with pain. I would like to express my gratitude and love to my baby, who made all this possible.

Maybe he will blame me for abandoning him someday.
Maybe he won't forgive me. Actually this is scary for me.

I am willing to take this pain, though, because he is
precious. His birth father also knows of his existence and
what has happened to him. He regretted what he had done.
Since I know how fragile a human being is, I have forgiven
him. Life is all about mistakes and regrets. I hope my boy
will understand that the father was not the wrongdoer but
we were all victims at the same time.

Now I am a housewife in my thirties. God had responded
to my prayers to marry someone who would accept my
past. I met my current husband, got married, and had a boy
who is four years old now. My husband and I are looking
forward to meeting my other son in the future.

I know I was extremely lucky and blessed. Most of you
adoptees probably don't know who your birth parents are
and cannot meet them. I understand this would give you
great pain and anxiety. Maybe you wouldn't be able to
forgive them for putting you in this difficult situation.
However, one thing is clear—you are very precious.

I know this because you are the ones your birth mothers
wanted to keep despite all of the obstacles. I pray for you so
that my tears can heal your pain even a little. Like a long-
awaited spring rain, I will be happy if this will give you a
little comfort.

I would like to finish my story with a gospel song I like:

You were born to be loved.
You are loved through every moment of your life.
The love of God comes to fruition through our ties.
How much happiness you bring us!
You were born to be loved.
And you are loved even now.

 A note from Sangsoon Han

This birth mother maintained a close relationship with Ae Ran Won after she left. For more than two years, she donated 30,000 won each month to help with the other mothers and babies. Then she visited me to say that she was going to get married, and the man was not wealthy, so she would have to stop donating for about ten years. But she gave me a white envelope, and said there was a small donation in it to buy diapers and food for the babies at Ae Ran Won. When I opened it, it had 1,000,000 won in it, which was a very generous gift. I told her that it was too much money to give Ae Ran Won, especially when she was about to get married. She finally convinced me that it was very important to her that Ae Ran Won have this money, so I agreed to put it to good use. In the time since then, she had another son with her husband, and has been leading a happy life with them.

chapter 6

$\mathscr{Y}$our Bright Future

(baby born in 1997)

My name is Jinyoung. I am the youngest of five children—
one son and four daughters—in my family. However, to be
more accurate, this is not my real family. I joined this
family, my biological father's family, after I had lived with
my biological mother for seven years. Even though my
mother had explained to me that I had to move in with my
father's family in order to attend school, as a young child I
did not fully comprehend her hidden message.

In the new household, I had a "big mother" (stepmother).
As I got older, I learned that my biological mother had met
my father while he was on a business trip to the countryside
where she lived. My mother eventually fell in love with him
and continued dating him with the hope of marrying him.
She did not know that he was a married man. She learned

about his marital status only after she became pregnant with me. Today, at the age of twenty-seven, I can imagine the level of shock and pain my mother must have felt when she learned that he was already married.

I began a new chapter in my life when I moved into my father's home. My life there cannot be described in words because it was just too painful and difficult. Since I cannot write in detail about all the events and experiences, I will write an abridged version. While I was sad to be living away from my own mother, I also was excited about the prospect of having older siblings. However, the reality was far from my expectations.

In the beginning, everything was awkward. Understandably, I was a real thorn in the eye of my stepmother. However, my step-siblings gradually accepted me as their youngest sister. I soon assumed all the household chores. As a nine-year-old child, cleaning the house, washing the dishes, and doing the laundry was difficult, and I really hated doing such hard work. It was a big relief when, on rare occasions, my older sisters helped me with the chores. At the time, I just could not understand why I, as the youngest child, had to do the entire household's chores. As I got older, I began to understand my situation better. My initial reaction to my difficult existence was to wish that my mother had not given birth to me or that my father's family had not taken me in so that I could have continued to live with my mother. Despite all the hardships, I somehow managed to graduate from junior high school.

I then left my father's house to attend a vocational high school. I worked at a factory during the day, attended school in the evening, and studied late at night while living in a dormitory. I was able to endure those difficult years, and still managed to graduate from high school, because I was already used to working days and nights while living with my father's family. Following graduation from high school, I decided to become independent. I rented a room with a friend and searched for any and all kinds of work. We somehow managed to get by.

Shortly thereafter, my roommate introduced me to a man. I dated him for five or six months, but we did not talk about our past lives. One night the man and I met for a drink, and we started to share our difficult life stories. I got carried away and became drunk. This was my very first time consuming alcohol. I soon passed out. The following morning, back at my place, I still felt the disorienting effect of the alcohol. The man unexpectedly came to visit me at home that morning. He proceeded to rape me while I was disoriented. I was so shocked by the absurdity of the situation. I just wanted to die at that moment and to be relieved of my deep pain and anguish. I had no one to share my agony with.

Soon after, I learned that I was pregnant. In a state of shock, I informed the man about my pregnancy. He gave me some money and instructed me to get an abortion at a hospital. At that point, I decided not to ever see him again, but I also realized that the only real choice I had was abortion. But when I arrived at the hospital, I couldn't go through the door. I just could not justify the idea of ending a precious life simply because I was not prepared to take care of it. I decided that I should save the life.

After much introspection, I informed the baby's father that I had aborted the baby, and I discontinued communication with him. While I was pregnant, I wondered how in the world I was going to support the baby as a single mother. Confused and helpless, I revealed my situation to one of my older stepsisters. After a lengthy discussion, my sister introduced me to an adoption agency, and with the agency's coordination I was admitted to Ae Ran Won. Living at Ae Ran Won, I met many other women in similar situations to mine, and I became more comfortable with it. We became very close as we shared our thoughts and feelings about pregnancy, delivery, and our babies' futures as if we were an extended family. As there were thirty-five of us living together, some had difficulty in adjusting to the communal lifestyle. Since I made an extra effort to help those women with the transition, I was able to make many friends and gain their respect.

At Ae Ran Won for six months, I was able to reflect on my life. Among the several useful programs offered by Ae Ran Won, I found the individual and group counseling sessions to be most helpful. The sessions gave me useful information that helped me think about my future as well as the baby's, and to make a wise decision for both of us. I was able to think and plan more realistically. Moreover, while attending church services there, I came to understand that I was not born to be scorned or despised but to be loved and respected. This realization gave me much comfort and strength. I decided to lead a life of a respectable and noble person. Therefore, I was baptized a Christian and I pledged to be celibate until I got married.

At Ae Ran Won, I was able to give my full attention to the baby because I was living a stable life for the first time. I ate well for the sake of the baby's health and was even given tablets to take care of my anemia. I even took a series of voluntary prenatal training sessions, with the hope of giving the baby an easygoing, happy personality. I read good books, walked while listening to pleasant music, and continuously told the baby how much I loved her. In this way, six months passed by very quickly.

During one of the counseling sessions about the baby's future, I decided to give up my baby for adoption. Even after making the decision, and on the way to delivery, I kept thinking about how I could raise the baby on my own. But I made up my mind firmly because I had lived a difficult life and I could not bear the thought of my baby living as an illegitimate child, as I had.

I was able to spend a brief, private moment with my baby after giving birth. Looking at the baby's angelic face, I was moved by the fact that the baby slept peacefully, without any worry, even though we would be separated forever in a moment. I wished for a continued peaceful existence for the baby. That is why I tried so hard to ignore the recurring thoughts in my head of how I might be able to raise her on my own.

It turned out that I was able to spend more time with the baby than expected, though, because the adoption agency unexpectedly delayed the adoption process. I wanted to keep my lovely baby at my side. While praying for good adoptive parents for the baby, deep inside, I still wanted to raise her myself. However, I also knew that such thoughts were driven by selfishness. I was not afraid of the suffering I would endure while raising the baby on my own. Rather, it was the social prejudice against unwed mothers and their children, and the suffering *she* would have to go through, that scared me most. I also feared the inevitable questions my child would ask while growing up in such a prejudiced society. I most feared being asked, "Why did you give birth to me only for me to suffer such misery?" I posed the same question to my own mother many times while I was growing up. I could not bear the thought of raising my child in such a difficult situation. I wanted to give her an opportunity to be raised in a more normal family environment. That is why I decided to give up my child and ignore my strong emotional pull.

The adoption workers asked me the universal question, "Why do you want to put up your child for adoption?" My only reasonable answer to such a question was that it is the best way to deal with my "reality." I did not like my reality and it took me a long time to accept that. I would have raised the child on my own if I did not think about her future—but I had to consider it. I could not sacrifice my child's future just because of my selfishness. Even so, regardless of the wonderful opportunities my child will receive as a result of leaving this prejudiced land, I am forever guilty in the eyes of society. It took a long time before I could even forgive myself.

An issue in Korean society these days is the very low birthrate due to women's refusal to have children, and the projected decline in population in the future. Ironically, the same society despises unwed mothers who want to raise their children themselves. Moreover, Korean society is very alarmed about the fact that Korea is the world's number one exporter of babies. Then why doesn't our society give opportunities and assistance to those unwed mothers who want to raise their babies on their own? Why does society not want to take a more active role? Is being an unwed mother who refuses to abort her child such a big sin?

Our society is full of injustices, especially toward unwed mothers. Even at an adoption agency, unwed mothers sense the sharp judgment and criticism cast upon them by looking into the caseworkers' cold eyes. Though their body language and facial expressions may hide it, their eyes cannot ultimately hide their disrespect. After all, you can read someone's true feelings by gazing into their eyes. As I write this story, the reality is—regardless of how much progress our society has made—that our society's negative attitude toward unwed mothers remains the same. While experiencing mistreatment, I came to a realization that we, the unwed mothers, must change our attitude before we can expect Korean society to change.

After giving birth and sending their children to adoptive families, all birth mothers, I am certain, have the same hopes and dreams for their children—that they will live better lives with the new families than with their own mothers. I had long dreamed to have a beautiful daughter one day. I then gave birth to a daughter. I could never have dreamed of the possibility of having to give her up. It was truly unfathomable and I had an emotionally difficult time after she was gone. Even though I had experienced a painful childhood, such pain cannot compare to the pain of giving my daughter away. I despised my mother, my father, and the whole society, but I hated myself the most. And I felt the heavy weight of guilt whenever I thought about my daughter.

Nevertheless, I wish for my daughter—while somehow absorbing the positive sentiment and good intentions of every Korean—to grow up to be someone who is thoughtful and considerate about the needs of others; who is always welcomed and needed; who makes a difference in society; and who is loved by her adoptive parents while being a source of happiness for them.

Most importantly, I hope she will come to the same realization as I did: that she was born to be loved and respected—not to be despised or deserted by her own mother. I do not know whether my child will understand my true sentiment, but I sincerely hope she will forgive me and understand that my decision to send her away was purely based on my unselfish love for her. I pray daily that all my hopes and dreams for my daughter will come to fruition.

I personally hoped for a large, extended adoptive family with grandparents for my daughter. I reasoned that if the adoptive family had grandparents, the family would likely foster a strong sense of respect, closeness, and fellowship. Then my child would naturally learn the right family values by observing her elders. However, my biggest hope is that she will become strong and never feel inferior just because she was adopted. I believe that she is much more fortunate being raised by a good, loving family in a prejudice-free society, than by an inadequate mother like myself.

My dearest daughter,

Somehow it has been a month since you were born.
You must have grown a lot by now. I miss you so much.

I presume you will harbor ill feelings toward me after you are all grown up. I ask for forgiveness from you, hoping that you will lead a happy life even though you will no doubt experience much pain and loneliness in the foreign land. You may even feel that I gave you up because you are worthless to me.

That is not true, my dear child. I love you more than anybody in this world. Forever. Although the labor pains were unbearable, your health was my only concern. I cannot adequately describe in words the pure joy I felt the moment you opened your eyes for the first time. You were such a beautiful little angel.

I regret not giving you more love while you were in my tummy. Before coming to this place, I was just too self-absorbed with my pain to even think about you. After arriving here, however, I tried to make up for it and gave you extra love. The time I spent with you after your birth is unforgettably precious to me.

My dearest daughter, please forgive me for sending you away. Despite the pain I went through in giving you up, I did it for your benefit and well-being. I hope you will cherish your life and accomplish whatever it is your heart desires.

I do have one request of you. I hope you will entrust your life to God, as I had met Him at the edge of the cliff. I make the following prayer to him:

> *Please release my daughter's pain unto me, so that her pain may be alleviated. Please pour unto her, like a waterfall, what I did not have before— freedom, joy, and happiness—so that she can lead a fulfilling life. Then all my past sufferings would have served their purpose.*

I would like to conclude this letter with my most sincere wish for your bright future.

From your very inadequate mother . . .

An accomplished cook, Jinyoung enjoyed volunteering in the kitchen at Ae Ran Won on weekends, making people happy with her food. And whenever the residents had to leave the premises to go on a picnic or attend summer camp programs, she would actively help and escort frail members to those events. She also took an active role in helping new residents adjust to the communal lifestyle.

Jinyoung also shows great leadership through her shining personality. At a festival sponsored by the Association of Women's Welfare Institutions in Seoul, she was instrumental in rallying Ae Ran Won residents to enter a talent show. Her group even won first place with a dance she choreographed herself. When she first solicited her friends to participate in the talent show, their response was, "How can we unwed mothers dare to stand on the stage without feeling shameful?" One by one, her friends changed their minds and participated in the talent show. Winning first prize enabled them to temporarily forget their sadness and be happy. Jinyoung changed the whole mood of the event from shameful to celebratory.

While she was living at Ae Ran Won, Jinyoung's stepsisters visited her periodically to give her spending money and to provide emotional support. They agreed not to inform her stepmother about the situation. During that time, the family was experiencing much turmoil because her father had left her stepmother for another woman. Of course, he also did not know of Jinyoung's situation.

After leaving Ae Ran Won, Jinyoung initially wanted to reunite with her previous roommate but changed plans and moved into her sisters' home because they gave comfort and strength. She also wanted to work as a hair stylist, but soon realized that such an occupation was not stable in the long run. Therefore, she decided to become a nurse and attended a nursing institute to earn her credentials. Becoming a pediatric nurse would have been an easier career path, but she also learned that she would always remain as an assistant with no opportunity for advancement, so she pursued a more demanding position at an OB/GYN practice. After gaining five years of experience as an OB/GYN nurse, she attained a career-track position in nursing. With her increased skill level, her income also increased.

After meeting a man two years ago, she fell in love and got married but has yet to share with him her painful past experiences. She is currently five months pregnant, and once the baby is born she intends to raise it with extra love and care to atone for her past action. Unlike in the past, she now lives in a socially secure and comfortable family environment.

chapter 7

$\mathscr{A}$ Move to Jeju

(baby born in 1997)

Hello, I'm Seong-Lim's mother. Let me introduce my story.
My father passed away when I was thirteen years old. I have
three older brothers and two older sisters. I'm the youngest
daughter. Even though my father died early, my
grandmother, mother, and siblings loved me very much, and
I grew up happy. My family wasn't rich, but there were no
financial problems. I lived in Kang-leung, Kangwon
province in Korea until I finished middle school. I moved
to Bucheon to go to a high school that is located in
Kyungkido, because my mother and grandmother wanted
me to continue to study close to Seoul.

I was a very self-sufficient girl when I was seventeen. I
started doing part time work such as babysitting, working
at a pharmacy and a store, and tutoring during every

vacation. I did my tutoring work until the third semester of college. However, on the fourth semester vacation, I went back to my hometown because I was feeling weak. During my resting time, I met my old friends, and one day we went to a restaurant. I met Seong-Lim's father there. He was a part-time cook. Even though he had a father, a mother, and his siblings, for some reason he did not receive enough love from his family. That was why I had motherly affection for him, because he looked lonely. We were getting close very fast, and wanted to get married. However I could not tell my family. I was still a college student, and my boyfriend was not ready to support a family. There was no way to get married.

But I got pregnant. At that time, the anti-abortion policy of the Catholic Church crossed my mind, and my family is Catholic. Because they are Catholic, I believed that my family would allow us to marry if we had a baby. I thought that I could use that. But Seong-Lim's dad rejected the idea of going to meet my family to ask if we could get married. Besides, I had severe morning sickness during my pregnancy, so I had to interrupt my education as well, because I couldn't stay at home any longer. Finally I began to live at my boyfriend's home. Even though it was a brief time, we were quite happy. I told my mother that we lived together at his place, but I didn't tell my siblings. My mom didn't know about my pregnancy at that time. I started preparing for an examination to be a public office worker, and he got a new job at an automobile service center. I was happy, but that lasted only a month and half. Then, for four months, we had lots of problems, and I used to faint because of the stress of the conflicts with him. He always projected a vague attitude and never said anything about our future and our baby. Therefore, we always kept on arguing over those issues.

It was unavoidable that I should return to my home alone. I told my mother that we broke up because of personal differences. I couldn't stay in my home, because my neighbors didn't know yet about my pregnancy, and they would probably shun me when they figured out that my body shape was changing. I didn't want my family to get into serious trouble because I was having a baby without marriage. So I decided to go to my friend's home in order to protect my family. Fortunately, my friend's neighbor introduced me to Holt Children's Services, which is an adoption agency, and they also introduced me to Ae Ran Won. In almost my ninth month, I entered Ae Ran Won.

If I had not had the chance to enter Ae Ran Won, I couldn't imagine my present life here and now. During the time before I entered Ae Ran Won, I was insecure, so I couldn't do any good prenatal care for Seong-Lim. However, my life was getting stable in Ae Ran Won for a month before Seong-Lim was born. Ae Ran Won was such a paradise to Seong-Lim and me.

What made me to decide keep my baby? I love babies, and it was my intention to raise Seong-Lim. It would be natural to bring him up. I had some money that I had saved from my part-time salaries, and I was confident that I could raise my baby by myself. However, it was urgent that I find a place where I could live and get childcare. It wasn't easy. Ae Ran Won provided a place where the mothers who keep their child can stay after they give birth at Ae Ran Won. But that place was already full with unmarried mothers and babies, so I couldn't stay there. A social worker at Ae Ran Won helped me move to another group home, another social welfare facility for women like me, but we couldn't stay there after about two weeks. The place was too cold— there was no heating system for the residents—and Seong-Lim was getting sick. We moved to my friend's home where I had lived before.

I let my family know about Seong-Lim's one-hundredth day. Even though my family members are religious as Catholics, they wanted Seong-Lim to be adopted. However, I stubbornly resisted the adoption issue, until finally they agreed with me. But I also agreed to an option that I should give Seong-Lim's father one more chance. So we lived together for two months, even though I realized that he neglected his duty as a dad and husband. After all that, my family approved of my decision to be separated from him.

Officially, my family accepted Seong-Lim and me as a family. I was very happy and appreciated my family. However, I didn't ask for any help from them. I wanted them to see that I could be stable and could live well as an unmarried mother. I didn't tell my family that we were moving to Jeju province, which is an island in Korea. It was possible to move to Jeju because my best friend lives there.

That was the time that I felt God helped us. My plan was well on its way to success. An acquaintance introduced me to a foreign company that had less prejudice towards unwed mothers. (At a job interview, the interviewers liked my attitude, which is dignified and bright even though I am an unmarried mother.) I found a childcare facility near my office that would take care of Seong-Lim while I worked.

Since then I've been working very hard. As I worked for the company, it was necessary to speak Japanese. I started learning Japanese. For a while, I couldn't get more than three hours sleep each night. But three years later, I could speak Japanese quite well and also contribute to my company. Fortunately, my efforts came to be recognized by senior officials and coworkers. My salary was increased, so I could be self-reliant economically, physically, and mentally.

I am satisfied with my life with my son. Seong-Lim is a nice, healthy five-year-old boy. Life is more stable than ever before. Of course, Jeju province is a unique place to stay, and it was very beneficial for me to move here. "Three abundance" is a famous saying in Jeju province. It refers to the three things that are abundant in Jeju Province: wind, rocks, and women. Here, people assume that women have more vital energies than men. Generally, women have the responsibility for their family finances. They have been involved in farming, or working as shellfish divers. On the other hand, men have been taking charge of households, and the care of their children. Jeju province has quite different customs compare to the main part of Korea.

As a result of working hard, I bought a house and a car. These days, I have a big change in my life. A man whom I've known for quite a while wants to marry me. He told me it is beautiful that I've been trying hard to keep my family healthy in such a difficult situation. My son also likes him a lot, and says he wants him to be his daddy. Because he understands, he will love me the way I am. What makes me think about marrying him more than anything is that he treats my son as his own.

I want to say thank you very much to Ae Ran Won, where there was support for me to give birth and raise my son, Seong-Lim. Thank you very much.

 A note from Sangsoon Han

In August, 2002, when Ae Ran Won held a conference called "How Can We Support Unwed Mothers and Their Children?", I asked this birth mother to be one of six mothers who would make presentations. She was very happy to do that. She came to Seoul, and spoke publicly about her story for the first time. She brought along her son, who was about sixteen months old at the time; her baby was on her back during her talk. Everyone there was very impressed by her and her confident attitude, and how she cared for her son. She helped them realize that unwed mothers can, indeed, raise their children. Now she is a strong supporter of Ae Ran Won. Three years ago she married, and now also has a daughter with her new husband, and they live happily together.

$\mathcal{A}$s Happy as Any Parents Would Be

(baby born in 1997)

I am a thirty-two-year-old woman. I live with my daughter, who is now in fourth grade, and my mother. As I look back on my past, I feel as though I am digging out something that was buried deep in my heart. I still feel an unbearable sorrow that has been perfectly hidden away, and which I pretended never existed. It's the past that I've been trying to put away, but today I am here to share it with you. I bring this out because there might be someone, even only one person, who might choose to hope and to go on after listening to my confession.

About twelve years ago I met this man at the college we both attended. We hung out together all the time, introduced ourselves to the families, and almost got engaged. I thought we were going to get married, but then he had to do his military service. During the service, he was severely injured and had to be discharged due to his injury. Once he returned, we moved in together.

When we had lived together for a couple of months, I found I was pregnant. Everything changed. It turned out that he was never ready to be a father. He told me that his family was happy to know that we were going to have a baby. He showed me a congratulation message. He showed me a savings account with twenty million won, and a lease that he signed for a place to live. But then he disappeared, and I found out all about his lies. All the things he had said were not true. By the time I confirmed all those documents were forged and fraudulent, I was due to give birth soon, and didn't know what to do. He obviously didn't want to be responsible for a baby, but kept that hidden from me for a long time.

My heart was torn out. I didn't feel like I could go on after all these betrayals. I was out of my mind and crying for days and nights. I thought I was a smart girl who knew what she was doing, but I wasn't. I couldn't believe what had happened to me. It felt unreal. It was so unfair. I was living dead. Then it was my mother who came to me to say, "Sweetheart, I am here with you, I'll be with you and I'll help you raise our baby."

I came back to my senses. I had to live for my baby and for my mother. I had my baby girl when I was twenty-two years old. But I couldn't register her birth on the family registry because her father and I were not legally married.

According to the officer in charge in the ward office, there seemed to be no way to register a birth without a father. I had to find the father. I was desperate to find him so that I could register my baby. Somehow I managed to find him and get him to officially marry me. Then I was able to report my baby girl's birth. I didn't realize what I was doing, and I didn't know what I was going to go through because of the marriage report. If only I had known another way to register my baby girl's birth back then, I wouldn't have done it. I should never have married him.

I did everything to make money to support my child. I am short and tiny, but I had to be strong. I got a day job as an instructor teaching students at a private institute and I worked at a restaurant at night. I had another part-time job for weekends. After a while, I was hired as a nurse/teacher in an orphanage to take care of children, and I was able to bring my own child to stay with me. Most of the children there were abandoned or given up by their parents. I spent a lot of time with the children, and I was a teacher, friend, and sometimes substitute mother for the children. They all had deep wounds in their heart. While I devoted myself to caring for these children, I myself felt cured and got healed from all those pains.

As my daughter grew up, I decided to file for a divorce from my legal husband, whom I had never seen again after we filed the marriage. I consulted a lawyer, but it was just too expensive—I didn't realize it cost that much money to file for a divorce. So I decided to handle it on my own. I defended myself. I started studying the family laws and it seemed to take forever. It was harder, because I was all alone. I had to file a lawsuit with no professional assistance. It wasn't even easy to fill out one form to turn it in. But finally, I submitted all the documents and went through all the procedures required. I made it and I was no longer married to him. I was free.

It had been long time since I left college, but I wanted to go back to study. I quit my job at the orphanage to be a student again. I was a mother during the day and a student at night. It was not easy, but I really wanted to be a mother who my girl could be proud of. I needed a full scholarship. Without the full scholarship, there was no way to afford the college tuition. I studied really hard and did my best, and I never missed being in first place.

After I graduated from college, I worked as a counselor at the sexual and domestic violence counseling center. While talking to those who were sexually abused and who suffered from domestic violence, I came to look back into myself. I learned a lot from them, and I had a chance to look ahead. It was a valuable time and experience because I started thinking about my own life.

I make about one million won a month, and I have a daughter and a mother to support. One million won is not enough to get by for the three of us. It's not easy. But I am the only one with an income, so I wanted to make it better. At the same time, though, I also wanted to be better than what I was. I wanted to do something and I knew what I could do. I wanted to help out children who were abandoned and hurt. I decided to study child welfare in graduate school.

The only way to afford the graduate school was to get a student loan. I studied hard. I devoted all my energies. I was under great pressure, both financially and psychologically. Sometimes I didn't feel like I could breathe at all.

I had a sixty-four-year-old mother and a little girl, both of whom needed me, and there was no one who could help me. To be honest, I suffered from an obsession.

One day, without any expectations, I submitted an application to a scholarship foundation. I made it to the final interview. After the interview, I got the scholarship even though, as I later found out, the scholarship foundation doesn't support students in the child welfare field. It was almost a miracle for me. I felt so relieved from anxiety and so thankful to God for the scholarship. I completely trust and rely on God, and it seemed that God was there with me to help me. I couldn't stop crying for a long time.

When I was pregnant, I had to stay in my room all day long to avoid others' eyes. I couldn't help getting caught by others' eyes. Back then I never thought that I could be someone. I remembered that I was addicted to smoking and drinking. I was an alcoholic. But now, I am different, I wanted to be a good mother and I wanted my girl to be proud of me. And I'll be a good mother to my daughter.

My girl is now in fourth grade. She is an adorable and lovely girl who likes singing and dancing much more than studying. I can't offer much to my daughter, like other parents do. But I am a happy mother. I am as happy as any parent would be, and when I pray to God, holding my daughter's tiny feet, I can't believe how happy and how lucky I am. I never did anything good enough to deserve such an amazing gift. Now I know that it is my responsibility to take care of her.

But I am not too sorry to her about not having a father. I try to explain to her that there are many different kinds of families in the world. I don't want her to know any of my bad memories of her father. I say, "A family with a father and a mother is not the only kind of family. Grandma, mom, and you is also a family. And there are many other kinds of families. They're happy, just like we are." I don't know how much the little girl understands, but she tries to comfort me. I know she has feelings against her father, but she has taken the reality pretty well.

Now I know that God was always with me under all circumstances. When I am in darkness, God always keeps me safe. I give thanks to God. "Thank you, God. Thank you for your grace and endless blessing. I'll give out to those who are in need, what I have received from you."

A note from Sangsoon Han

The writer was not from Ae Ran Won. Later she joined to Ae Ran Unwed Single Mothers' Support Center (http://www.singlemom.or.kr), which was established to support unwed single mothers and children in 2006. She has been sharing her stories with Ae Ran Won residents in a group counseling sessions that help them make decisions for their babies' futures. The story above is what she prepared for the speech, and she agreed to share it with readers of this book as well.

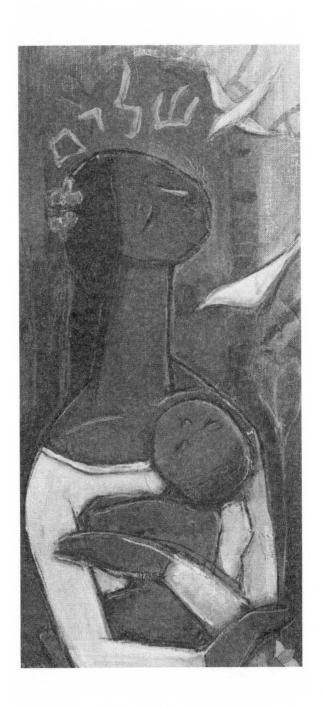

$\mathscr{W}$orse Than a Criminal?

(baby born in 1998)

Hello! First of all, I would like to greet those of you who are reading my story.

Several years ago, I was an unwed mother who had to give up a beautiful infant daughter for adoption to a family in the United States. I now write this story as a lawfully married mother of two children—a three-year-old boy and a seven-month-old baby girl.

The reason I've chosen to write my story is that I wanted to explain why I put my baby up for adoption. I realize that some people might think that I'm writing to placate my guilt, but that's not true. I recently read a newspaper article about international adoptees who had a difficult time coping with their sense of abandonment and lack of understanding over why they were given up. I was hoping that my story might offer them a glimpse of what life is like for many birth mothers who do not have the option of keeping and lovingly raising their own children, even though they would like to. However, I certainly don't expect those who read my story to agree with the decision I made, nor am I hoping to generate sympathy.

I was born into a troubled family. Most people I know in Korea remember their childhood and adolescent years as times of school, parental love, and friendship. For me, though, these were times I would rather forget. My parents fought virtually nonstop and more or less neglected me, so I looked to my older sister as both a parent and as my only friend.

Living in that home environment, drawing was the only activity that gave me solace and peace. Drawing was everything to me in those days, as it also gave me the strength and confidence I needed to cope on a daily basis. However, my parents wouldn't even allow me that little shred of happiness, saying that I was wasting my time. While I was at school, they would tear up all the pictures I had drawn at night. Sometimes they would even come into my room and take the drawings away after I had fallen asleep. Being at home became increasingly unbearable, so I started going to a local church to be in a more positive environment. But even that did not last very long. Since neither of my parents believed in religion, they were adamantly opposed to my going to church.

After spending my childhood and teen years in such an unhealthy environment, I finally graduated from high school and immediately started working. I also resumed going to church, without my parents' knowledge. I could no longer bear living with my parents, so, at the urging of a friend from church, I left home on a cold winter night. Since I didn't have anywhere to stay, and was not earning enough to rent a room, I decided to stay in a small storage room at my church. I couldn't even keep in contact with my older sister and most of my friends because I didn't want my parents to find out through them where I was. I had lived in this way for six years by the time I turned twenty-five.

That period of my life was filled with loneliness and sorrow. Despite the hardships, what kept me going was the strength I drew from God. In the best way I knew how, I tried to learn and grow from the teachings of Christ, so, in many ways, those days were very special to me. At the same time, I was so caught up in my own survival and self-pity that I didn't have very good interpersonal skills or judgment. My maturity, confidence, and inner strength were not where they should have been, considering how old I was at the time.

Despite trying to stay strong, I was so lonely that I often cried in envy and longing when I saw seemingly happy families in my neighborhood, especially at night when I could see them through their apartment balconies. "I bet those people don't fight and resent one another. Had I been born into one of those families, I might have been able to go on to college to study drawing," I would say to myself. I would console myself by believing that the happiness and acceptance that seemed to elude me would sooner or later come my way. I desperately wanted to believe that, because hope was all I had going for me.

It was around that time that I met the man who would shatter my life.

He was an employee of a company close to where I worked. We had known each for about three months without much interaction, but once we had a chance to have tea together, our relationship developed rapidly. We went from being mere acquaintances to friends, and before I knew it, we were talking of getting married. I had never experienced so much happiness. He took care of every meal, called me endlessly on the phone, and took me wherever he went. I was so intoxicated with happiness that I loved, accepted, and believed everything about him. I would do what he asked, including having a physically intimate relationship. Since we were going to get married soon anyway, I was not worried about becoming pregnant. Carrying a child of the person one loves is not only natural, but a blessing as well, or so I thought. I found out I was pregnant eight months after we had begun dating.

Strangely enough, even before I told him the news, he suddenly, and without explanation, severed all contact with me. Since no one knew him very well, including his former coworkers, I was unable to get in touch with him. Still, I wanted to give him the benefit of the doubt, so I waited for him. I was exactly two months pregnant then, and could already feel the baby growing inside of me, so giving up hope was not an option. A few months after his disappearance, I found out that my boyfriend was actually a married man with two sons. What's more, he had amassed a huge debt from constantly borrowing money from his coworkers and anyone else foolish enough to lend him money. This included some of the people I worked with, who had discovered all this about him while looking for him when he had failed to pay them back.

By that point, I was six months pregnant and had no idea what I was supposed to do. He used to introduce me to his friends and colleagues as his girlfriend whom he would soon marry. Because he had told me he was a devout Christian, we had shared many long conversations about God and our faith. How could that man have been a married father of two? I had not once doubted him, but it all turned out to be a big lie. At first, I had trouble believing what people were telling me about him, but soon, reality sank in and I realized what a fool I had been. I was completely devastated and lost.

As far as I knew then, no one knew about my pregnancy. I hadn't even told the pastor and his wife at my church— I was very close to them—because I had planned on telling my fiancé first and then sharing the news with everyone else. Because it was my first pregnancy, I hadn't gained much weight and my belly still wasn't conspicuous. But time kept flying by and the baby grew steadily, so I knew that everyone would soon discover the secret I'd been trying so hard to hide. Feeling desperate and full of regret, I could not forgive myself for having been taken for a complete fool.

I spent day after day in tears, while battling depression and insomnia. When I tried to pray to God to pull myself together, I could only feel anger and resentment. How could you have done this to me, God? You knew this was going to happen, but instead of guiding me, you just abandoned me. It was bad enough I was never loved by my parents, but what is your reason for dropping me into this abyss? At the very least, you could have helped me by spontaneously aborting the baby at the onset of my pregnancy! I alternated back and forth between cursing God and beseeching him to help me find a way out, but he didn't seem to be listening.

Since I couldn't allow myself to bring a fatherless child into this world full of intolerance and misery, I wanted to have an abortion even though it was already too late. But once I saw my baby's peaceful image on the ultrasound screen and heard his heartbeat, I just couldn't go through with it. For once, I realized how sacred and precious human life was. I could still hear the doctor saying, "Congratulations! Your due date is August 26." All of a sudden, it dawned on me that God must have had a reason for everything, even for the child I was carrying. Since God had already given me the gift of life, I figured there must be a silver lining in my situation as well. I began praying to God for his guidance every step of the way.

By this time I could no longer conceal my growing belly, and my coworkers started whispering and snickering behind my back. Some people openly criticized me, saying that I was a prostitute who would sleep with anyone, and they treated me accordingly. Some male colleagues even went so far as to boast that they had slept with me. Those who weren't as openly critical would stop their whispers and giggles whenever I appeared, and then resume as soon as they thought I was out of sight. The thought of quitting my job had crossed my mind on countless occasions, but I didn't want to give those people the satisfaction of seeing it as an admission of guilt. In fact, I became determined to prove them wrong, and decided I would quit only after changing their opinion of me, even though I had no idea how to go about it.

At my church, people began asking whether I was ill, so in desperation, I told them that my failing health was causing my stomach to become bloated with fluids. At that time, I was working as a Sunday school teacher and was a member of the church choir. The thought of my pupils' parents finding out about my pregnancy was frightening because they would have stopped sending their kids to me, claiming that such an immoral person should not be allowed to teach and influence their children. I was also certain that the choir would force me to leave. The church had been my only refuge and I could not risk being driven out. I was willing to endure all the humiliation and contempt at work, but I was much more afraid of being disowned by my church community. If I were to lose that, I didn't think I would have a reason to go on living. Despite the guilt I felt, I went on deceiving everyone at my church.

The time passed, and soon I was approaching my due date. In preparation, I scheduled five days off from work before and after my delivery date. As much as I had wanted to think straight and stay focused, I was out of my mind from anticipation, fear, and nervousness. The closer it got to the due date, the more fearful and frantic I became. I desperately longed for someone to stay by my side and help me get through the ordeal even though I was used to taking care of myself and being alone. Then, around ten o'clock on Saturday night about ten days before my due date, I began experiencing a severe stomach pain similar to menstrual cramps at thirty-minute intervals. For a short while, I failed to understand that this was the signal of the start of labor, but when the cramps began occurring at ten-minute intervals around midnight, I finally realized that the baby was about to arrive.

I quickly grabbed the bag I had packed and the large amount of money I had set aside for the hospital fee, and went to a small, privately owned hospital close to where I lived. In the waiting area after checking in, a nurse gave me some forms to fill out and asked me about my family situation. When I informed her that I was an unwed woman without a family, she asked me whether I had the money for the delivery. I handed her the envelope containing the money. She told me to wait a bit and went away, but soon came back. She handed my money back to me and told me to go to another hospital. The hospital refused to admit me because I was an unwed woman with no guardian present. I couldn't believe what I'd just heard, but there was no time to protest as the contractions became more forceful.

I could barely walk, but I had no choice except to find another hospital. After about ten minutes I found one in the area, a bit bigger than the one before. It never occurred to me that two hospitals would turn me away in the condition I was in, but the second hospital treated me even worse. I felt anxious and fearful as I told my baby, "Please, little one, hang in there just a bit longer." By then, even more forceful contractions had started coming at five-minute intervals. I was in so much pain that I could hardly understand what the nurses were saying to me. But once they found out I was not married, the tone of their voices and attitude took a sharp turn—they told me to stop whining because other women could endure the delivery pain just fine so I needed to step up to it. I still wonder how they would have spoken and treated me had I been a married woman with family members at my side.

I was devastated. I called up an acquaintance, a former coworker with whom I hadn't been in contact for a long time, and told her what was happening. With no hesitation, she and her mother rushed to the hospital and offered to be my guardians for the night. I felt so much more secure and was at last able to lie down on a delivery table. Just as I was feeling a bit relieved, the doctor in charge of the hospital came and told us to leave, saying that he couldn't accept non-family members as my guardians. In disbelief, I told him that the baby was just a push away and begged him to let me deliver, but to no avail—he said that I was in good enough shape to find another hospital nearby. He even got irritated and angry at my friend and her mother when they started pleading with him as well, and yelled at all three of us to get out at once.

When we left the second hospital, I was no longer able to walk. My friend's mother carried me on her back until we hailed a cab. We then went to a much bigger hospital. Unlike the first two, this hospital admitted me. I was rushed to the waiting area of the delivery room. I was determined not to leave again, no matter what, even if it meant delivering on the hospital floor. As I waited to be taken into the delivery room, the events leading up to that point went through my mind. I found it hard to believe what had just happened—and the Korean government and its people claim that this country has joined the ranks of the developed nations? Unbelievable!

It began to dawn on me that I was nothing more than a criminal and a sinner in the eyes of society, despite my efforts to hold myself together, despite my belief that this life I was carrying inside me was a gift given by God. I had always thought that hospitals were places where people were supposed to be treated and taken care of. Even imprisoned hardcore criminals receive medical treatment or surgery when they need them, and yet I was treated worse than the worst of society by two hospitals in a row, just as I was about to deliver a baby! In the eyes of this unforgiving and condemning society, this baby I was about to bring into the world would be nothing more than the illegitimate trash of an equally worthless mother.

Little one, I'm so sorry. The problem isn't so much bringing you into this world, but all the pain and discrimination you would have to endure for the rest of your life. This society will put a label on you the second you're born. When I think about that, I can't bear to bring you into this world and I don't want to. I am so sorry! The hospitals wouldn't even help with your birth, so I can't even imagine what the rest of your life would be like. I can't do that to you, and I no longer have any hope or faith left. Please forgive me, little one. I am not going to push you while you attempt to come out. Just accept your fate in my womb because I feel that's really what's best for you. Please understand that I'm doing this because I love you.

Dear God, what have my baby and I done to deserve this treatment? Have I committed such a big sin? Even criminals receive treatment and operations when they fall ill, but is being an unwed mother a greater crime than what they've done? This is all too difficult to take, and I pity this child. Why, of all people, did you have to give me this child? You could've given this child to a loving family that really wants a baby, but why did you choose me of all people? Please allow me to let this baby die. I implore you.

While these thoughts were rushing through my mind, my face was covered in tears. I clenched my teeth and didn't push as the contractions became even more urgent. The doctor in charge of my delivery was instructing me to push, but I ignored him and went on talking to my baby in my head. "I'm sorry, little one. I hope you don't try to live much longer. You must resent me for giving up now, but I think that this decision is really what's best for you and me. I'm sorry." At first, the doctor had thought I was simply having difficulty coping with the pain, so he tried his best to relax and comfort me, but he soon sensed that something else was amiss.

He went outside to ask my friend and her mother to persuade me. When he came back into the delivery room, he told me that even though he could sympathize with my reasons for refusing to push, I was jeopardizing my own health as well as seriously endangering the baby's life. He even scolded me gently by telling me to stop thinking only of myself. Even if I didn't want to give birth, the baby would come anyway, so I might as well make it less difficult and painful for the baby, as he had already suffered enough, the doctor said. I realized he was right, so I began pushing.

Ten hours after the labor began, I gave birth to a baby girl. I fell asleep soon after and didn't wake up for almost a day. Once I woke up, I wanted nothing more than to see my baby, even though I could hardly move. At that point, my friend came into the room with some underwear for new mothers and other gifts. She said she'd already seen my baby in the newborn room and had even talked to the doctor who had helped me deliver.

My friend was clearly disturbed by what she had seen the night before and how the baby was doing. According to her, because I had refused to push and delayed the birth, the baby had swallowed too much amniotic fluid and her own feces, and was having difficulty breathing. The doctor had told her that I would be allowed to leave the hospital in three days, but the baby needed to stay for further observation and treatment. I was struck at once by the guilt of knowing that what I had done was unforgivable. Thinking about my child either dying or living the rest of her life in a disabled condition made me go crazy, and I hated myself for having been so selfish and thoughtless.

I was able to walk the next day, so I went to see my baby. She was lying in the newborn room amidst other babies. Recognizing my own baby wasn't hard because she was the only one with a noticeably wrinkled dark skin covered with hair. Other mothers were allowed to pick up and hug their babies, but mine had what looked like a huge needle inserted through her skull. I was so devastated by that sight that all I could do was cry and apologize to my baby over and over. As I dragged myself back to my room, I realized that I needed to think very seriously about my baby's future. The first thought to come to mind, of course, was to raise her on my own, but once I realized how much discrimination and pain she would have to endure, I just couldn't. Instead, I wanted her to go live in a country that values human rights, like the United States.

As soon as I was released from the hospital, I went directly to an adoption agency and informed them of my decision. An arrangement was made for me to relinquish my daughter to the agency as soon as she was released from the hospital with a health clearance. Then I went back to the hospital with an adoption case worker and a foster mother who would take care of my baby until her departure. At that time I was able to hold my baby in my arms for the first time. My hands and heart trembled together. Despite my determination to not cry, I couldn't help myself once I saw her sleeping peacefully in my arms with her tiny hands and fingers clasped.

My little one, I am so sorry. I hope you will understand why I am sending you to a better place. Should you ever decide to look for me, I want to be there to meet you without any shame—I hope you decide to come and look for me some day. I love you.

While holding her for the first and last time, I cried for what seemed like an eternity. Then I let her go. The adoption worker who had come to the hospital asked me to name the baby, but I declined. I had no right to such an honor after trying to kill the baby, so I asked the adoption agency to choose a Christian name for her. The baby was given my last name, Choi, and she was named Eunhae, so she became Eunhae Choi. And she was gone.

My breasts were severely swollen, but there was no baby to feed. Just when I thought things couldn't get more difficult, they did. How I wished to have breast-fed her even once. I also worried whether Eunhae would cry in discomfort because she somehow instinctively missed having her mother's milk. I should have held onto her a bit longer . . . I nearly went insane going over such pointless thoughts. If it hadn't been for my belief in God, I probably would have killed myself out of depression.

When I went back home, the pastor and his wife from the church came by with a big pot of seaweed soup, which is given to new mothers, and a few other side dishes. They told me that they had known about my pregnancy since I was about three months along, but hadn't said anything because I hadn't approached them about it. I was so grateful for their thoughtfulness and discretion. Having someone like me at their church might have tarnished their reputation and ideals, but they embraced me rather than judge me.

My baby was sent to the United States six months after I had given her up. Shortly after, her case worker gave me an envelope containing photos of Eunhae from her new home. She had transformed from a newborn with hairy and wrinkly dark skin to a beautifully glowing angel with a bright smile. Even though I clearly knew that she was gone, I would sometimes hop in a cab heading for the airport with the thought that I might be able to see her one last time if only I would hurry. I just couldn't let go. Then on the way to the airport, I would decide to return home, chiding myself to snap out of it and pull myself together. I didn't want to be someone my daughter would be ashamed of when she returned to find me.

To regain the life I had, I even resumed going to work. Unfortunately, people kept their distance from me because I had left a bad impression on them. They still viewed me as no better than a prostitute, and some of the male coworkers would even approach and bluntly ask me to sleep with them. But after having gone through the experiences I had had, I could not let myself fall apart, so I tried my best to ignore them and concentrated on focusing on my job, home, and church.

A year later, a matchmaker came to me with several proposals. Even though I wanted to get married, if the man had never been married, I declined. Because I had already given birth out of wedlock, I didn't think it would be fair to a single man to have to marry me, so I wanted a match with someone who was looking to be remarried.

Finally, the matchmaker came to me with a proposal from a man with two daughters in grade school. He was looking to get married again, so I agreed to meet him. Once my coworkers found out that I intended to meet the man, they chastised me by saying that I should be thinking about bringing back the child I had abandoned rather than trying to become a mother to someone else's children. In their eyes, I was not qualified, nor did I have the right, to be those girls' mother. That was the straw that broke the camel's back. I could no longer endure being in that hostile and unforgiving environment. I had hoped to change my coworkers' opinions of me with my dedication to work and professionalism, but that wasn't to be. Shortly after, I changed to another job where people didn't know about my background.

That's where I met my husband. I was upfront with him from the beginning about my past while we dated. We have now been married for four years and have a three-year-old boy and a seven-month-old baby girl. I've since patched things up with my parents as well. In fact, our relationship has improved so much that hardly a day goes by without one of us calling the other. As before, church plays an important role in my life. Since marrying me, my husband has been attending the church that has been like a true family to me.

For a while after giving up Eunhae, I thought that I would never find happiness or acceptance, but I was wrong. Eunhae has given me the strength to go on and make something of myself. Whenever I get depressed and find life hard to cope with, I think about the day we will meet, and that alone changes my outlook by breathing positive energy and strength into me. All I can do in the meanwhile is to hope that she's growing into an amazing human being in God's care. Whether or not she chooses to look for me later, I've begun preparing myself for that possibility. For starters, I am studying conversational English because I have so much to share with her and I want to hear all about her life. I'm also planning on getting a simultaneous translation certificate. And should Eunhae's adoptive parents choose to visit Korea with her, I would be honored to be their guide and translator.

I thank God for giving me the gift of hope, guidance, and health. I also pray for the health and well-being of Eunhae and her family members in the United States. I live each day hoping and praying for the day we meet again. Today is Eunhae's sixth birthday.

Written by Kyung Hwa in Seoul
August 16, 2004

A note from Sangsoon Han

Kyung Hwa asked to use her real name for this story, because she is very interested that her story be in this book. She was not originally a client of Ae Ran Won, but she heard about this book project and asked if it would be OK if her story was included. I was happy to have her story in this book.

$\mathcal{A}$ Double Loss

(baby born in 2000)

It has already been three months since I came to Ae Ran Won in the midst of my pregnancy, but it seems like only yesterday. I will think and try to write how I came to where I am today.

I was just an ordinary person. I was the elder of two daughters, and my family did not have any difficulties with finances. My mother was cautious, unlike my father, who was very strict and controlling. If I didn't listen to my father, he hit me severely. My younger sister was very studious and excelled at everything, so my father always compared me to her. I grew up with my father favoring my younger sister and hitting me. I always feared my father, and since I was rebellious from a young age I repeatedly ran away from home. Because of that, I was not able to do well in school. I dropped out when I was a senior.

I got a part-time job to support myself, and I cut off all contact with my family. While I was living on my own, I met the father of my baby. He was sitting next to me when my friends gathered to celebrate my birthday. He was eighteen and a student. We drank a lot of alcohol and had casual sex while drunk. We kept in contact, and later I learned that I was pregnant.

When I first missed my period, I thought that it would come the next month. I never considered that it might be a pregnancy. But after four months, I noticed that my stomach was expanding even while my period still didn't come. I went to the pharmacy to buy a pregnancy test, just in case. It was positive. When I saw the test results, suddenly everything in front of me became dark. But at the same time, I thought it was all right. No, honestly, I was happy. I started to cry with happiness, thinking of the tiny life breathing inside of me.

I was happy, so I called the baby's father with the news. But the father just told me to abort the baby. I was angry and disappointed, but for the sake of my baby I swallowed my pride and called again. The father told me to abort the baby and he would pay the hospital bill. In addition, his parents called me and yelled at me to abort the baby and not ruin their son's life. Then they hung up. At that time I was overcome with anger and decided to abort the baby with the father's money.

But I was afraid, and unable to go to the clinic by myself, so I summoned my courage to tell my mother both about the pregnancy and the reaction of the father's family. My mother clung to me and cried. I was so sorry. After that, my mother took me to an obstetrics clinic. I received all of the prenatal tests and saw my baby on the ultrasound. I was so happy at seeing the tiny form breathing and the tiny heart beating inside of me that I started to cry. My mother also began to cry. Even so, she insisted that I needed to abort the baby in order not to ruin my life. My mother promised to pay for the abortion. I was so ashamed of causing trouble to my mother that I couldn't beg her not to force me to have an abortion. Before we finished talking, I went with her to the clinic.

I was afraid when we were in front of the abortion clinic, and the image of the small baby inside me kept appearing in my mind. I was an emotional shambles. The baby had already taken a place in my heart. I begged my mother one more time to please let me give birth to the baby and raise it. What parent can refuse her own child? My mother loved me so much that she could not refuse my plea. I was extremely happy. I felt as if I had received the entire world.

From that time, I began a careful lifestyle. Before I knew I was pregnant I drank, smoked, and took cold medicines. I wanted to quit everything, but I couldn't manage to quit smoking. I learned from reading and from Ae Ran Won prenatal classes that smoking is bad for the fetus. However, someone else told me that it was all right to smoke just a little. I had had such a difficult time trying to quit smoking

that I listened to that person's advice and continued
to smoke.

Later, I went again with my mother to the clinic and asked
for help. The doctor told me that raising the baby would be
disastrous for everyone involved. He urged my mother and
me to tell my father of the pregnancy. At the time, though,
I hated my father and had moved out. Only my mother
knew where I was living. I was terrified that my father
would accuse my mother of not raising her daughter well,
and that he might beat her or even kill her. My mother
proposed that she and I should raise the baby together, but
that would have brought misfortune to our family. The most
important fact, however, was that I thought I could not
become a mother. I had no faith in my ability to raise a
child. How can anyone expect an eighteen-year-old to raise
a baby without a father? After deep consideration, I decided
that I lacked the qualifications to become a mother.

When I told this to the doctor, he advised me to put the
baby up for adoption rather than commit the murder of
abortion. He also recommended that I go to a place that
helped unmarried mothers like me. He told me, "You are
the best mother. You are giving your baby the gift of life.
No matter what anyone says, you are the best mother.
You are giving the baby all the love you can, and you are
doing your best for the baby." I came to agree with the
doctor. Because I was giving birth to the baby, I was giving
it life. So I decided to enter Ae Ran Won and place my
baby for adoption.

When I first entered Ae Ran Won, everything was strange and a little intimidating. I worried that I wouldn't be able to adjust to the regulated lifestyle here, but I tried my best. With time, I slowly became comfortable with the lifestyle and I got close to my roommates. I even made some friends. My friends and I occasionally got scolded for breaking the rules, but we also rose early in the morning to clean, took turns helping the cook and serving rice in the cafeteria, and participated in various activities. I occasionally became frustrated with difficult situations, but it was still a good experience. This was the only place that could offer me rest, a community of women in the same circumstances as me, and advice from my caseworker. In one word, it felt like *home*.

The obstetrician determined that my delivery date was in early May. I was overflowing with happiness as each day my baby quickly grew inside of me. However, I was worried because the doctor told me that the baby was very small for its age, and that it was also in reverse position. I diligently attended prenatal exercise classes and did the exercises recommended by the nurse, hoping that the baby would return to the right position. However, I was told that the baby needed to be delivered by C-section. I was afraid, but I kept thinking that I would soon be able to see my baby.

I hadn't been able to complete my schooling, but I received private classes from volunteer tutors, and I hoped that I would live well for my baby. Before, I had hoped to leave Ae Ran Won immediately after childbirth, but after receiving counseling I found the strength and hope to become educated and to live well for my baby. I was so grateful for the encouragement to study that I wanted to learn well. Even though I couldn't be a model student and always acted as if I weren't satisfied, in my deep heart I was very thankful.

While living in this way, I experienced labor pains greater than I ever had imagined. Two weeks before my delivery date, I called 119 (same as 911 in the United States) and went to the hospital. I immediately went into the surgery room, and my restlessness gave way to anesthesia. On May 16, 2000, at the age of eighteen, I gave birth to a baby son weighing about five pounds. It seemed like just yesterday that I had happily passed my hand over my pregnant belly, but already I had become the mother of a newborn son. Time had gone fast. After nine difficult months carrying my baby, I was happy.

While I am writing these words, the image of my son keeps appearing before me. When I was with my mother at the obstetric clinic four months after I learned of my pregnancy, my mother asked the doctor to show her the baby one more time on the ultrasound. She looked at me. She said that the baby's head, hands, feet, heart, and complete body were miraculous. She listened to the tiny heartbeat. We couldn't help crying together.

But that happiness passed by in the briefest of moments. I will explain why. I would like to say something to all mothers and pregnant women who are reading these words.

After the surgery, someone woke me up. I felt extreme pain as soon as I opened my eyes. The person asked my mother, who had been sitting next to me and caring for me, if my mother had seen the baby. My mother cried and said that the baby was very ill. The baby had birth defects. He had two fingers on one hand, three on the other, defects of his spine and genitals, and he needed an oxygen mask in order to breathe.

My world collapsed around me. I thought I would go crazy. I was in anguish. I wanted to die. But one part of me thought that perhaps my mother was telling me a lie so that I would not want to see the baby. I continued to think this way until I saw the baby.

My mother asked if I wanted to hold the baby, but at first I said that I would not. The next day, I wanted to see my baby and went to the nursery. But I couldn't make myself say that I wanted to see my baby. After a while, I gathered courage to tell the nurse my name and ask to see my baby. I put on a white gown and entered the nursery.

There were so many babies. I immediately noticed a baby with yellow hair, skin white like snow, and an oxygen mask attached to his face. That was my baby. My mother had accurately described his birth defects. But even so, he was still my beautiful baby. For a moment, it felt that my heart was torn in two by agony. What would it be like for him when he grew up? He couldn't grab with his fingers and cry. The image of him being teased by other children kept coming into my mind. When I thought of his days to come, it seemed like there would be nothing but despair. I had felt pain when I woke up from the surgery, but it was nothing compared to the anguish I felt now. In this case, it seemed my baby would be better off dead than alive.

My mother spoke to me in my anguish. She said he would grow up well and that no one would be able to kill my baby, even in this difficult situation. All right. My mother's words were right. Even though his body was not normal, it still was a precious life.

After experiencing various kind of pains, I was discharged from the hospital and returned to Ae Ran Won for post-delivery care. There, everyone asked me, "Is the baby pretty?" "Whom does he resemble?" But I couldn't bring myself to talk about the baby's deformities. Honestly, I felt ashamed. I didn't tell the people around me, but I did tell my roommates and close friends. I needed comfort. They gave me a lot of comfort and cried with me.

I was still recuperating at Ae Ran Won when I went to the hospital for my baby's discharge. He was wrapped in a carrying blanket, but someone took him out of the blanket so I could hold him. How was my heart, that minute I held him?

It was the first time I had held my baby. He had such a pretty smile. We got in the car and went to the adoption agency. When we went into the temporary nursery, there were many babies. They all cried to be held. I felt so sorry for them. However, I thought how wonderful it would be if my baby were healthy like those babies. I gave my baby to the worker and said a brief good-bye. I told him to grow big and healthy. When I had to leave him, I ached as if my heart were torn. It was so sad to turn my back and leave my baby.

I returned to my life. Many times, I was so anguished thinking of my baby that I couldn't bear it. I wailed and cried like a crazy person. I tried to think of how I could apologize to my baby. I had one thought: There were so many babies and not enough workers, so I thought I would volunteer at that place. I thought it would be a way to ask forgiveness from my baby. I also would live a proper life, for my baby.

Now I am living at Ae Ran Won, preparing for my future by studying and receiving training to be a hairdresser. After I finish my study, I will get a job, work hard, and help unfortunate people like my baby. In that way, I will repay my debt to my baby and my mother. Even though my baby is not able to be physically cured, I pray every day that he will be able to grow up healthy. I have faith. God will not forsake my baby, and he absolutely will take care of him. I also will live well so that I will not again disappoint my mother and my social worker. I am trying my best.

I want to say something to those reading my story. If you really love babies, please don't spend your nine months of pregnancy foolishly thinking "It will be all right." Cigarettes, alcohol, and other drugs are absolutely bad for the unborn baby. Please, please take my story to heart and remember my pain.

I am so grateful to my mother and the caseworker at Ae Ran Won. Because of them, I am able to smile brightly and have hope for my future. I am thankful to Ae Ran Won for helping unmarried mothers like me to be safe, not to give up on ourselves, and to have hope. I don't know how long I will be here, but while I am here I will try to do my best in everything.

 A note from Sangsoon Han

After writing this essay, Miss Ahn worked very hard hoping that her efforts to continuously live a good life would somehow help her baby's health. She prepared for the general equivalency test and learned the methods of hairdressing. Of course, she quit smoking. Whenever she lost her focus, she thought of her baby and strengthened her resolve to live properly, no matter how difficult it proved to be.

But on July first, about fifty days after the baby's birth, we heard that the baby had died from lack of oxygen. The adoption agency called us, saying that they were leaving for the baby's funeral, and they were wondering if we also wanted to go. Miss Ahn wanted to go with her baby to the very end, and as her social worker, I went with her. I asked Miss Ahn's mother if she wanted to go, too, but she was working in a restaurant, earning money to repay the costs of caring for Miss Ahn, and said it would be difficult to take the time off. It seemed to me, though, that she declined because she couldn't face going to the baby's cremation. Miss Ahn and I went alone.

We took a taxi to the hospital morgue. After going past a lot of trash and boxes in the dark, we came to the door of the room where the bodies are prepared. Inside, there was a box with the container for the baby's body. A baby inside a cardboard box tied with string. The casket was loaded into the hearse, and we went to the crematory in Kong province. After driving for about thirty minutes, the driver kept looking at us strangely as Miss Ahn and I were sitting next to the casket. After we arrived, a man wearing athletic clothes brought a stretcher. We put the casket onto the stretcher and followed him, but people were looking at us strangely. Because we had received the news so quickly, we had not been able to put on black clothes. We were following the stretcher.

Miss Ahn was not a legal adult yet, so I filled out the crematory paperwork for her. After just over an hour, the baby returned as little more than a handful of ashes. We went to Homodont Mountain to scatter the baby's ashes and pray for a peaceful life in heaven. The hearse driver took pity on us and kindly drove us back to Ae Ran Won.

In the car, Miss Ahn leaned against me and sobbed continuously. Even though she cried, she couldn't feel that the baby's death was real. She also seemed gradually to become more vacant. For three weeks after the baby's funeral, she returned to Ae Ran Won as before to take care of herself. But it was not as easy as she thought. She didn't have the desire, and she wanted to give up all her studies and leave the facility. Miss Ahn received the permission of her mother to return home. A few weeks later, she returned home and began to work in a beauty salon. Even though she kept her pregnancy and childbirth a secret from her father, his attitude toward her had not changed. She had such a difficult time that her mother rented an apartment for Miss Ahn close to their house. Miss Ahn lived there and worked at the salon.

While receiving the utmost love and care from her mother, Miss Ahn is slowly overcoming her grief and guilt about her baby. She sometimes visits the Ae Ran Won homepage and leaves a message about her current situation. She wants to live a good life, thinking that this is the only way to redeem herself with her mother and her baby.

$\mathcal{M}$aintaining the Connection

(baby born in 2000)

I decided to write a long apologetic letter. This letter is not a confession to God, not an excuse to justify my sin, but written for one person: my daughter whom I love the most in this whole world. This is a story I want to share with my daughter when she's older, when she's ready to hear me.

I'm currently attending college and will turn twenty-five this year. I was born to strict parents in an ordinary household outside of Seoul and, for twenty years, I was brought up as an obedient daughter who didn't cause any trouble. We weren't exactly rich, but still, I was active and cheerful and got along well with friends. Since I was in good academic standing, my parents and teachers had high hopes for my future.

For the first time in my life, I had to be away from my parents and live alone in Seoul because I was planning to attend college there. I wasn't scared. But, despite my optimism, I became lonelier as time went by. Individualism dominated college life and that added more loneliness to my life away from home. Instead of getting better with time it just got worse, day after day. Aside from attending classes, I would spend all day in the tiny rented room I lived in—only a few square yards in size—waiting for my boyfriend's phone call, which was the only hope and joy to me at that time.

I met my boyfriend, who is the same age as I am, at a church in my hometown. I was attracted to him because he had strong faith and leadership, and we started dating at the end of our sophomore year in high school. Both of our parents knew about our relationship and we were dating with their approval. We were each other's comfort and support in an unfamiliar city, Seoul. But unlike me, my boyfriend adjusted to college life well and he was busy everyday going to school and working part-time. He was unable to make as much time for me as I hoped for—to listen to my problems—and because I was so emotionally dependent on him, I felt like he was acting cold-hearted.

The only time I was able to sit down with him face to face was from midnight, when he ended his part-time work, till morning. He was living alone at the time, and we mostly just listened to each other's stories or watched television together. And then one day, he started demanding sex. At first, I adamantly refused. But as time went by he continued to request it. I loved my boyfriend so much and got scared thinking about the possibility that he would leave me if I continued to decline his demand. Looking back now, I know how foolish I was, but at that time, he was absolutely essential in my life. I was ready to do anything for him as long as he stayed by my side.

Unfortunately, my boyfriend didn't have any knowledge about birth control, and because I was extremely ignorant about sex, our relationship became very much one-sided. He steered the way and just dragged me around. After we started having sex, I became more dependent on him and more sensitive about things. But hardly three full weeks after we first had sex, my boyfriend wanted to break up. I hung on to him relentlessly, but he merely avoided me, making all my efforts to reconcile useless and futile.

Less than a week after the abrupt breakup, I found out about my pregnancy. I was so scared and frightened, but had no one to talk to. So I asked my boyfriend for help, but he also panicked and didn't know what to do. At last, I revealed my secret to an organizer of the Christian Club at my college and, through his wife, I was introduced to a priest who helped me bring my daughter into the world.

Admission to college, having sex for the first time, an unexpected breakup, meeting with the priest—all these things happened over the course of a month. I was confused and terrified. All I wanted to do was deny the reality of the situation I was in. I couldn't bring myself to consult even my best friend about what was going on. For me, there was nothing to do except cry alone. At the beginning of the pregnancy, I didn't eat for a week, and I cried all day. Alone in my room, I wavered between having an abortion and giving birth, until my mind went blank from pouring out all the tears in me. I think I shed all the tears of my lifetime during that period—that's how hard it was for me. Continuing day after day took so much of me that I just wanted to die.

I blamed God, demanding, Why is this happening to me? And I blamed my boyfriend, who avoided me even more after finding out that I was pregnant. But no matter how much I tried to find excuses for myself and blame others, in the end, it was me who had behaved in an irresponsible way. How can I be pregnant, such a good Christian girl? If word got around, there was no way I could attend church and school as if nothing happened. It would be even worse if my parents found out. It broke my heart to imagine their disappointment and pain, especially when they trusted me so much.

I couldn't tell anybody, suffered alone, cried myself to sleep, and had constant nightmares that even made sleeping a problem. Forcing myself to be hardened, I thought about abortion and even went to the hospital, alone, but had to turn back. I just couldn't do it. *I* was the sinner, not the small life growing inside me. I was so sorry, beyond words, to my baby.

My baby, when I saw her through the ultrasound picture, was so tiny and pretty. I knew I could never have an abortion. My precious baby. Upon deciding to give birth, I stopped going to school temporarily and lied to my parents, saying that I was going to the United States to study English. With a help of a priest from a pro-life organization, I stayed in the States for a while and came back to Korea and entered Ae Ran Won.

Many people helped make me able to come to Ae Ran Won. But I was unable to laugh wholeheartedly. Not even once. Because my sin was so immense, I thought I had no right to be happy. My grudge against my boyfriend led me to distrust people in general. Eventually, I met young souls whose situations were similar to mine, or worse. Through their bright and beautiful hearts I was able to open my closed and cold heart, little by little.

I was full of anxiety because my pregnancy was a secret from my family and friends, but as time went by, I thought of no one and nothing but my baby growing inside. Before going to sleep, I would put my hand on my stomach and talk to the baby for an hour. During regular checkups, when the doctor would assure me of my baby's good health, I'd thank God, without even realizing it, for sending me the baby, and ask him to protect my child.

Life, I realized, was full of constant obstacles. After deciding to give birth, another decision was waiting for me. I had to decide on whether to keep the baby or give her up for adoption. I couldn't rely on my boyfriend, who did nothing but avoid me altogether. I attended group counseling sessions at Ae Ran Won, to help make a better decision about the baby's future, and had weekly counseling sessions with the social worker and the priest. Yet I couldn't make up my mind about adoption.

People make unfair assumptions about unwed mothers. They're perceived as sexually loose women who irresponsibly abandon their own kids. It's easy for people to be judgmental because they're oblivious to the sleepless nights of sorrow and tears a mother has to go through, every step of the way, from discovering the pregnancy to making a decision to give birth.

People at Ae Ran Won, including me, cried again and again before deciding on adoption. No matter how young or immature you may appear to be, nobody was spared from that agony.

Someday my child would find me, her biological mother, and might ask, "Why didn't you raise me? No matter how hard it was, how could you give up your own kid? Then why did you have me in the first place?" I probably can't say anything at all because even "Sorry" seems so inadequate and would come off as an excuse to justify my actions. I'd probably just cry and cry.

But what I want to say when that moment comes is this: I want to say that I agonized over it, time and time again. But no matter how I looked at it, I had no alternatives. At one point, I felt like I could do anything as long as I could be with my baby. My precious baby who lived inside my belly for ten months—if I had to give up everything I own to be with my child, I said I could, that I would. But in the end, I didn't want to ruin my child's future because of my selfish desire. I didn't want my child to be branded as a "child of a single mother" in Korea, a place still overflowing with conservative and judgmental eyes.

"I love you, but there are so many hurdles we have to overcome for us to be together. I don't mind getting hurt, but if you get hurt, if you get hurt because of people's prejudice, I would prefer my own death over your pain."

That's what I would tell my child—that because she's more precious than my own life, I had to let her go.

Maybe from the very beginning it was as God planned in order to protect the life of my child—meeting the priest after conceiving the child, coming to Ae Ran Won, giving birth after twelve hours of intense labor, and the first time I laid my eyes on my baby.

Just like the meaning of her name, "Child of Jesus," because she's a child of Jesus before being my child, I felt like I had no right to be greedy. I wanted my child to be raised in a better environment, with more love, under the protection of God. And with much pain, I was able to make up my mind about adoption.

Even after deciding on adoption, my mind was unsettled. Yet, amid the torrent of confusion, deep down I felt a strong conviction. I knew that, because my child is blessed with God's mercy, God would prepare her path. And God showed me the path he had prepared. I wished for open adoption so that my child could find me whenever she needed me, and I also wished that she'd stay near me, not in some faraway place abroad. God granted my wishes and sent adoptive parents who prayed for my child since the beginning of my pregnancy. They were with me throughout my pregnancy and when I gave birth, and I knew from deep down that they would love and care for my child wholeheartedly. It's been five years since I sent my child to them, and I have no doubt in my heart that I made the right choice for my child.

People at Ae Ran Won envied me for sending my child to adoptive parents in Korea. And on top of it, it was an open adoption. I was very fortunate, for such cases are rare.

I wanted very badly to be with my baby for the first five days after the birth. They said that after five days a baby's umbilical cord usually fell off and I was desperate even to have that.

My child's adoptive parents suggested that I stay with my child at their home for five days. At first I hesitated, no matter how much I wanted to. I wanted to see how they lived but, on the other hand, I was worried that they might dislike my baby because of the disappointment derived from my pathetic state. But with good hearts they kept insisting, and I was able to spend five days with my child. When my baby's umbilical cord finally fell off, I kept it and brought it back to Ae Ran Won.

For the first year, I was able to visit their home once a month to see my baby. Such things rarely happened, even in open adoptions in Korea, and I feel truly blessed. To this day, I keep in touch with the adoptive parents on a regular basis, and when I miss my child I sometimes talk to her over the phone without revealing that I'm her biological mother. The adoptive parents are truly good people and they don't mind me visiting or calling my child. Furthermore, they encourage me to come and visit them more often. I bow my head and thank them from the bottom of my heart.

My child's father was on leave of absence at school, right before I gave birth, and entered the army to serve his mandatory military service. He had suggested overseas adoption, and I could tell that he was suffering, too. I told him that the child was adopted in Korea, and furthermore, it was an open adoption. Later, I heard from the adoptive parents that he visited their home to see the child during his short vacation from the army.

Right now, because the child is still young, she doesn't know the facts about me or the meaning of adoption. But I have thought about the child every day from the moment I gave her up for adoption. I worry about the child's reaction when she finds that her loving parents are not her biological parents, that she was adopted. What kind of face will she make in front of me, the biological mother, and what will I tell her? She may hate me and find it difficult to forgive me. But still, I hope from the bottom of my heart that she'll seek me when faced with obstacles in life, when in doubt of her identity.

Despite the fact that my child was adopted into an ideal family, letting go was extremely difficult for me. I couldn't function, even in daily life. My head was filled with doubts and regrets. I kept asking myself, "Did I make the right decision? Is it too late to turn back now?" I suffered from depression and anthropophobia. I was unsettled for a long time. Then one day it dawned on me that if I continued in this way, someday my child would grow up and visit me and see that my life was a mess. There was no way I was going to let that happen and bring sorrow to my child's heart. I said to myself, "Get up, be stronger. Study hard and one day show your child how healthy and stable I am." For my child, I had to pull myself together. And the fact that she was under the same sky, breathing the same air, gave me enough comfort to let me live again.

I recently finished college and am now preparing to get a job. I have no idea what kind of light will be shed on my life but, regardless, I am gathering my strength to go on thinking of my child. And I'm going to try my best not to hurt or disappoint my child in the future when she comes to see me.

Lastly, this is what I want to tell my child and to all the children who are adopted: "I didn't give you up because I didn't love you. From the moment I had you till this very moment, I loved you. I loved you, still love you, and will love you for the rest of my life. I was unable to live with you but there wasn't a moment when I didn't think of you. I'm always with you, I always will be. I love you. I love you. I love you. I can confess this hundreds, thousands times over and over again. I love you—truly, with all my heart."

A note from Sangsoon Han

Miss Yu is very pretty and thoughtful. She puts others before her with sincere humility and is beautiful both inside and out. As Miss Yu's assigned social worker, I was able to be with her throughout the difficult time when she made an important decision for her baby. At first, Miss Yu seriously considered raising the child herself. She asked me to convince the birth father to help her raise the child together. She thought that if he helped her raise the child, as a family, there would be the slight chance of persuading her own father, even with his temper, to support her decision.

When I met with the birth father, he said they couldn't raise the child because they were no longer together. Furthermore, he was strongly against the idea of Miss Yu raising the child alone. And he pleaded with me to persuade Miss Yu to consider only international adoption. He said that at first he wanted for her to have an abortion, but changed his mind after talking with the organizer of the Christian Club. He added that he was going to leave school temporarily to fulfill his military service.

Miss Yu was very disappointed. We put our heads together and discussed possible ways for Miss Yu to keep the child without the birth father's participation. If Miss Yu decided to become a single mother—give birth, and raise the child alone—her biggest concern was her father's reaction. Miss Yu was very much aware of his infamous temper tantrums and was afraid that he would blame everything on her mother and torment her. More than anything, it was this concern—her father and grandmother blaming her mother for not raising Miss Yu right—that caused her to stall. Life for

Miss Yu's mother was already hard enough, in Miss Yu's opinion. Her father and grandmother were drenched in Confucian traditions that brought great hardship to her mother.

After giving it long thought, Miss Yu chose adoption in Korea, which was rare and almost impossible. But her desperate wish was granted, for she was able to find ideal adoptive parents in Korea. The wife of the club organizer at Miss Yu's college, whom Miss Yu confided in after finding out about her pregnancy, asked a family she knew to pray for Miss Yu. And they constantly prayed for Miss Yu and decided to adopt her baby if she decided on adoption.

Miss Yu wanted to be with her baby after giving birth and the adoptive parents kindly allowed her to stay at their place while she recuperated. Miss Yu considered their offer with much thought and finally decided to accept their invitation. For her baby, she thought it would be best if she saw how they lived, and get to know the adoptive parents better as individuals.

On the fourth day of Miss Yu's recuperation at the adoptive parents' house, the adoptive mother called with an urgent plea for my help. She said that Miss Yu had been crying all day, continuously, holding the baby in her arms. When I saw Miss Yu at their house, I couldn't believe my eyes. Her eyes were bright red like a rabbit's eyes from crying endless tears. Capillary vessels around her eyes were broken and her face was bruised black and blue. I barely recognized her pretty, familiar face. As soon as she saw me she ran to my arms and continued to cry. Miss Yu said that she couldn't stand the thought of leaving her baby, which was to happen the next day. She added that she didn't want to waste even a minute not looking at her baby, and that she wanted the baby's face to be etched in her heart. She said she wanted to cry out loud whenever sorrow attacked her, making her heart burst into pieces, but she had to hold back her tears because she was scared that it might frighten the adoptive mother and the baby. She was afraid to disappoint the adoptive mother, for she was worried that such judgment would influence her love for the child. Miss Yu confessed that holding back her tears was very hard and that she thought dying would be easier.

I told her to let it out and cry all she wanted to. Holding onto me, she cried again, and after a long cry she wiped her tears and said, "I'm okay now. Crying out loud made me feel better." She graciously thanked me for coming to visit her. She predicted that her baby's umbilical cord would fall off the next day, and that she would leave this place and return to Ae Ran Won soon. Referring to the umbilical cord, she said, "I consider myself lucky, for I can take a part of my baby with me."

The next day the adoptive mother wholeheartedly urged Miss Yu to stay longer, but Miss Yu insisted that she wanted to keep her word. She thanked the adoptive mother for her kindness and came back to Ae Ran Won to complete her recuperation. Miss Yu stayed at Ae Ran Won and helped teen mothers with their GED, right up until her own school started.

As the first day of school approached, Miss Yu e-mailed her parents that she was returning to Korea and went back to her hometown. Miss Yu's father rented two rooms in Seoul for Miss Yu and her younger sibling, who was about to start college. She returned to school but couldn't overcome her guilt and emptiness. She couldn't eat anything and started drinking. She would drink heavily, get drunk, and cry, which startled her friends. And because of her drinking, Miss Yu developed a stomach ulcer. For one semester, Miss Yu's breakdown continued. Every time things got tough, Miss Yu came to me and cried. And even during the most difficult of times, she always visited the baby once a month. To help her, I introduced Miss Yu to a birth mother who had lived at Ae Ran Won in 1996 and had put her child up for open adoption in the United States. This woman also spent the first several years suffering from the loss of her child. Since her child was in an open adoption program, she received detailed progress reports and pictures of the child's growth. For her, confirming that her child was safe and happy helped her overcome feelings of loss and anxiety. And for Miss Yu, this birth mother became an emotional and spiritual mentor.

Soon after, it was the baby's first birthday. Several of us from Ae Ran Won met Miss Yu near her school to celebrate the occasion together. After dinner, we searched for a place where Miss Yu would be able to cry freely. We finally decided on a karaoke singing room. We thought she'd feel most comfortable knowing her crying wouldn't be heard by other customers singing loudly in their rooms. We settled down and put a candle in the cake I had prepared. We sang the birthday song for the baby and Miss Yu blew out the lone candle with a smile. Then she cried for quite some time, and we sat by her side, holding and consoling her. We took pictures, and told her that when the baby grew up and later asked, "Did you think about me after putting me up for adoption? Do you still love me?" she could show these pictures and tell the child, "I met with close friends and thought about you as we celebrated your birthday." We cried together and laughed together that night. Miss Yu said that if she were alone she probably would have been drinking to ease the suffering and pain. She said she felt fortunate spending her child's first birthday with close people who loved her.

That year, however, Miss Yu's father was forced to retire from his job. This put the family finances in dire straits, and her parents told her they couldn't continue to send her tuition and living expenses. So Miss Yu's younger brother gave up going to college and instead enlisted in military service. Miss Yu took a leave of absence from school. During this time, Ae Ran Won searched for a sponsor who would cover Miss Yu's education costs and, as a result, Miss Yu received support through the priest who had helped her earlier. Miss Yu continued with her studies while making her own living expenses through a part-time tutoring job. I cannot reveal Miss Yu's major here, but around this time, I also found out the old computer she was using lacked the capacity for her school assignments. I informed her church sponsor about this situation, and soon after, Miss Yu was overcome with joy that she could buy a new computer. It brought me much happiness to see her happy, too.

Miss Yu eventually graduated school. She has found a job and lives a stable life. And her life's goal? Her child calls Miss Yu "Auntie" right now, but when the day comes for her child to understand Miss Yu's true identity, Miss Yu wants to be in a position to stand proudly and unashamed.

Not long ago, Miss Yu called and told me there was something she really wanted to do with me outside Ae Ran Won. On my way to meet her, I wondered what it was that Miss Yu wanted to do so urgently. As soon as she saw me, Miss Yu asked when I had last seen a movie. I laughed, saying, I couldn't even recall. Her eyes brightened as she told me she prepared an event for me since I was always buried in work without a chance to enjoy any cultural activities. She had been waiting for me with two reserved movie tickets. We watched the movie together and had a marvelous time over dinner, too.

As Miss Yu looked back on her life, she said, "If the baby was adopted overseas or in a closed adoption program in Korea, and if I couldn't meet the child anymore and make sure she was safe and happy, I don't know how I would've overcome that harsh difficulty. So I'm very grateful that my child is in an open adoption in Korea." She also said that it was possible because people around supported and encouraged her, which made her who she is today. In the past, she was unable to forgive the birth father and even herself, which caused her to abuse herself. But now, she has reached a point at which she can forgive the child's father and even herself. Miss Yu's last words to me that day still whirl in my ears: "Now, when I walk on streets and see children the age of my own, they're all precious and beautiful in my eyes. I think I can now forgive both of us and love again." I was happy hearing her say this.

In the Spring of 2009, Miss Yu married her boyfriend, and now lives a happy life.

A further update by the Korean adoptive mother

*A Special Present, My Second Daughter, our baby's birth mother (29 years old)

At ten p.m., the news finally arrived. Ae Ran Won contacted us to let us know the mother went into labor and was moved to the hospital. My husband and I rushed to the hospital. We promised an open adoption for her baby and planned to stay by her side as she gave birth before we received our baby. My heart was pounding and the anxiety was overwhelming as my husband and I arrived at the hospital around midnight. She was lying on the bed alone. I thought to myself, she must have endured so much difficulty and faced tough times alone, until now. My heart went out to her.

It was our first meeting. She was a pretty mother and I thought our baby would be very pretty, too. I chastised myself for harboring such selfish thoughts during a situation like this and I greeted her. I also felt bad, because I wondered if I could ever be more to this young mother than a person who came to take her baby away. I felt all the more sorry because she was a mother who was resolved to raise her child for the baby's sake, despite her own future and outside criticism. For twelve straight hours the labor pains continued. And even during labor, the mother was praying. Keeping watch by her side was exhausting as it was; I could only imagine how much worse it was for her to be going through the pain. Our faces were a mixture of sweat and tears, and it was only after the thin blood vessels in her eyes and neck broke that she was moved to the delivery room. As we waited outside, time seemed to stand still. All we could do was pray:

"Dear Lord, please help us. Since You protected them until now, please save them." Between my ongoing sobs and whimpers, people passing by asked who I was crying for. I said it was my sister, and really felt that way.

At last, finally, the baby was born. Our baby was so beautiful when we gazed at her with our tearful eyes. She had fair skin, big eyes, double eyelids, cute dimples, and rolled her large sparkling black eyes as she surveyed the world. And before long, she fell asleep. What a precious life! I felt apologetic that this child was almost lost to abortion in the beginning. The baby was so peaceful. The nurse asked if the baby was being sent to an adoption agency, and my heart brimmed with pride and joy as I replied "No." I was so grateful to the young mother for allowing us to be by her side throughout the night, and for letting us partake in the inspiring moment despite her immense pain. I felt dizzy thinking we might have missed the birth of our second daughter. And thankful that it wasn't lost time, that I'd be able to tell my daughter later on, "When you were born . . ."

After spending two nights at the hospital, we were given permission to bring the baby home. The birth mother decided on adoption during her last month of pregnancy and wanted to stay with the baby for about five days after birth—just until the umbilical cord fell off. I felt strange and worried that parting would be more difficult if the birth mother became attached to the baby, or that she might change her mind about adoption. But I soon realized it was a blessing for our baby to have the birth mother nearby, that there was probably no place more peaceful for our newborn than to be held in her arms. I also wanted to witness this peaceful scene and asked that postpartum care take place at our house. I was happy that there was something I could do for the baby and birth mother. I was also thankful we could bring both the baby and birth mother back home together, and that the baby could rest in the birth mother's arms. The birth mother suffered from constipation and her swollen breasts. I was worried that they might cause her further complications or suffering. One thing after another would come up, but I admired how the young mother endured it.

The promised five days were passing and even though we insisted she stay longer, she adamantly said she'd leave on time. She said she just wanted to see the baby's umbilical cord fall off. How distressed she must have been, on the fifth and final night, as she slept with the baby. She couldn't even cry openly in front of the baby girl, for fear it would trouble her. It wasn't until later that I found out, but she said the child cried so much that she stroked her eyebrows while lulling her, cooing, "Don't cry. You won't be loved if you keep crying." How must her heart have felt? As if consoling the birth mother, our daughter's umbilical cord fell off the next day, and the young mother asked for my permission to take the cord with her.

What must her heart have felt as she wrapped it carefully as a keepsake. I, too, am a mother who gave birth and raised a child, and couldn't help crying with her because my heart constricted, thinking about the birth mother's pain of having to leave her child behind. We went to the adoption agency together and she waived her parental rights in writing. We received permission to take the baby home immediately. We drove the birth mother back to Ae Ran Won and she said her farewell to our daughter. There seemed to be so many hurdles the birth mother had to overcome. And she would endure more and more each time. There were so many difficult moments. I never understood that this process would be so challenging. And I regretted my previous assumption that adoption was an easy decision or option for unwed single mothers.

She said it was more difficult to cope after sending the child to the adoptive parents. That it was like carving out your own flesh. The baby would cuddle in the birth mother's bosom, breast-feeding, or cooing, and crying. That scene was the most beautiful and lovely in my eyes. And it is a priceless fortune for my baby and me. Even now, I still feel apologetic when I see the birth mother. I encouraged her to visit whenever she wanted to see the baby, instead of repressing her desire. And fortunately, my husband left for a business trip, which created an opportunity for the birth mother to visit again and sleep over. This visit offered me some consolation since she left so abruptly last time. When the director of Ae Ran Won requested a writing piece, she mentioned that it must be difficult being this considerate to the birth mother. But the truth is that anyone would do the same if they were in a similar situation. No, wouldn't they have been more considerate?

Later on, the birth mother continued to visit us once a month. I'm thankful that she gave birth to our second child and comes to visit every now and then. Many a time I'm confronted with people asking, "Aren't you nervous about her continuous visits?" But in reality things aren't like that. I take great joy in seeing our daughter with her birth mother, and in being able to see the birth mother make progress in recovery. Listening to her talk about her experiences while she was pregnant with our daughter gives us a sense of stability as well. We're happy to share the baby's happy, settled, and lovable new life. I organized the baby's pictures I prepared beforehand to give her. I told her to hold on to them, so when our daughter became curious about her birth mother and visited, she'd be able to show them to her and talk about these days she shared with us.

Our baby, already six months old, has been crawling here and there. She's been busy playing with her sister, who is twenty-two months older than her. I haven't seen a child this beautiful around me. When I see the birth mother, I always feel apologetic that I'm the one raising such a beautiful child. And our daughter is so easygoing—she makes my job such a breeze. In fact, I've received more from our second daughter than what I've given her. As a mother, I haven't been able to do anything extraordinary or special for her, yet she loves me so much. Every time our eyes meet, her large pentagonal eyes and exceptionally black pupils sparkle at me as her smile widens. Even if she cries because of strangers, when I pick her up in a tight embrace she stops right away and shows off her bright smile. When she wakes up from her slumber, I'll usually find her playing on her own in the crib. Her chubby arms and legs are so adorable and she's become quite a chatterbox as of late, even though it's all gibberish. When my husband and I are crouched out of her sight, she'll pull herself up by grabbing onto the crib railing and yelp out with glee when she finds us right there. Sometimes, she feels silly and plays little pranks on us, too. When I see her playing on the bed, my heart expands at this most precious and beautiful sight. I hope my daughter will grow up to take pride in her own identity, be respectful and thankful toward her birth mother, and live a happy life in this world.

$\mathcal{T}$o Grow Up in the Light

(baby born in 2001)

Hello! I'm an unwed mother. I am raising a five-year-old
daughter. When I was twenty-five years old, I was working
for a company, living a normal life. I had a boyfriend.
He and I loved each other. He had a much better family
background and education than me, so I did not even
dream of marrying him. And then I got pregnant. I told
him that I was pregnant. I tried not to push him, because I
did not dare to want to marry him. Anyway, he did nothing,
other than tell me that I should take care of everything. We
hurt each other and eventually broke up.

My heart ached when I thought about my baby. But I had
not thought about giving birth either. I thought it was
almost like suicide to be an unwed single mother. Several
times I went to a small obstetrical hospital to have an

abortion. But I could not bring myself to have the procedure done. Instead, I just had medical related checkups. One day I saw my baby's ultrasound photo and the word *abortion* just went out of my mind. Friends pushed me not to give birth. Being an unwed single mother meant giving up my work and disconnecting from my family.

At the time of my pregnancy, I was working for a general hospital. The hospital had a regulation that states if an employee does harm to the reputation of the hospital, the employer can require the employee to resign. I knew being pregnant before marriage was against the regulation. So I quit on my own before I was told to resign, and I tried to find a place to stay until I gave birth.

I had never really thought about the idea of an unwed mother, but I searched the Internet for that term. And I found out about Ae Ran Won, which was a facility for unwed mothers. I was counseled by an Ae Ran Won social worker about topics such as how long I could stay and what kind of help I could get. I did not have the courage to talk about these things to my family. Even if my family understood my situation and accepted me, I was afraid that other people would look at my family differently. People like to judge others negatively, so I didn't tell anyone except my sister and then entered Ae Ran Won. Before long my family knew what had happened to me. They were shocked. My father said that he would not see me anymore, and my stepmother kept sighing and crying. One lucky thing was that my parents were Catholic, so they did not insist that I have an abortion.

Even though I was brave my first time entering Ae Ran Won, I soon could not take even one step outside the three-story building. When I had to pass by the front door I walked very fast because I was afraid that people outside could see me. I kept condemning myself and was afraid of meeting people. But I took many different kinds of programs—yoga class for pregnant women, parenting education, Bible study, needlework, flower arranging, and individual and group counseling—and I started to change.

At that time I had not thought about adoption. I was not really even aware of it. I was thinking only about bringing up my child. But how could I bring up my child if I kept isolating myself from the outside world? So I decided to try to get out as much as possible. I was told by a social worker that Ae Ran Won provided job search programs. I started to go to a dressmaking institution. That class was held only twice a week. Little by little, my self-confidence was being restored and I could afford to think about not only my past and present but also my future.

I was planning to go back home after giving birth. But I knew that my parents were fighting often because of me. I dropped by my home now and then. But every time I visited my family, they felt very uncomfortable. They were ashamed because other people were either hostile toward us or were curious about our situation. So staying home even for a short time became a hard thing.

Time went by and I gave birth to my daughter. I was not fully prepared for this change and I suffered severe postpartum distress. I remained bedridden for a month and was cared for by volunteers and postpartum helpers. A social worker told me about Ae Ran Seumter, a group home run by Ae Ran Won. At Ae Ran Seumter, unwed mothers could prepare themselves to stand up on their own financially, socially, and emotionally, as well as receive job education. The social worker said I could get more professional dressmaking education, which I was glad to hear. I could then get a job in that field, and at the same time get help related to bringing up my child. I took the good opportunity that was given to me.

I moved to Ae Ran Seumter when my daughter was two months old. I was so thankful to Ae Ran Seumter because it gave me a hand when I did not know what to do and had no place to stay. Ae Ran Seumter supported me in many ways. Not only did I get a place to stay, I also got powdered milk and money to help me raise my baby. I also got information about welfare programs so I could send my baby to a daycare center for free. There was a nice social worker who always took care of me. I received a lot of benefits and help even though I did not feel that I had earned it.

After a year at Ae Ran Seumter I graduated from a professional job school. I studied fashion design and passed a certification exam. But I wanted to study more. Of course, I could have managed to earn my living with the certificate, but I had a bigger dream. I remembered the director of Ae Ran Won once said that she would support anyone who wants to study at a university. I asked the social worker to find out if that promise was still valid.

The answer was yes. So I applied to a university's fashion design department and was admitted. Now I am preparing to graduate soon from the university, thanks to tuition support. Recently it was my turn to enter Mojawon, a home for mothers and children that is supported by the government. So I am staying there. At my university I studied really hard. I got more certificates than other students got and always did my best to get good grades.

Some people have criticized me, saying that I should be working instead of studying. They said that I have no sense and do not understand my own situation. I don't think they are necessarily very wrong. But I think studying is an investment in the long term. This opportunity became possible thanks to the support that was given to me. If I did not study or did not have any skills, I, an unwed single mother, and my child would have a dark future. My body and soul would get poorer and poorer and my child would be influenced by that environment. I do not expect I will find a decent job right away. But one thing that I'm sure of is that I will have more options than I had three years ago.

I still face many obstacles. Just doing my best is not enough to deal with obstacles such as the problem of childcare when I have to work late, or the struggles I have with people and society because I am an unwed mother.

But I think that I have been really lucky. I was blessed enough to be able to bring up my child myself and get a chance to be educated. How many other people have been blessed as much as I have been?

If I had not come to Ae Ran Won, and then to Ae Ran Seumter, I would have gone to my family, which wasn't ready to accept me. I would have been miserable and guilt-ridden about my parents fighting because of me, and would have had a hard time getting a job. So I truly wish that other unwed mothers who choose to bring up their babies will have the same opportunities as I had.

When I become friends with someone, that person always tells me something like this: "You are so brave. You are bringing up your child on your own. If I were you, I could never have been like you. But don't tell other people that you are an unwed single mother. It is not good for you. If they already know about you, it will be okay. But if they know that you are an unwed single mother before they know you as a person, they will not want to be close to you. Getting a job will be difficult too. You know what society is like. It's okay only inside school." Professors, classmates, and other acquaintances are all the same in saying that. I also know well the disadvantages of telling people that I'm an unwed mother, because I have been through all these things. But I don't want to hide my child in the shadows any more. I chose to raise her rather than place her for an adoption, and I want her to grow up in the light, not in the dark where she will be disconnected from society.

I am sometimes praised for bringing up my child. Many people say, "If I were you I could not have done the same as you. You are so good!" Up until seven years ago, I continued to believe I had done well as an unwed mother because I felt I had done better than other people. However, I soon realized it was not because of that.

I had a friend at Ae Ran Won with whom I stayed. She had chosen adoption and felt thankful about that choice. How? Why? I did not understand her, so I used to tell her, "It would have been better if you had brought up your baby. Kind and composed women like you should bring up their children." One day she dropped by my place and said that she was so proud of me. She told me about another friend she had who was an unwed single mother. And, she added, she wished that friend had been like me.

The story of that friend is like this: "She went back home, which was in the country, after she gave birth. She was so afraid that other people would know that she was an unwed single mother. She knew that in small towns like her hometown everyone knew about everyone. She was afraid of going out of her home, so she and her baby never went outside the house for six months. It was very hard for her to be locked in a house so she moved to a place close to her sister's. The place was downtown, away from home. But she still was afraid of what people would think of her, so she kept herself in the house and felt hopeless. She gave up everything and became obsessed with the thought that no one would accept her. She lost self-confidence, too. She was too devastated to love her own child. As a result her child was not being raised well. Sometimes such horrible thoughts came into her mind like, It is just because of that child . . . I wish I did not have that child . . ."

So my friend's friend regretted her choice to keep her baby. Both mother and child were having a hard time. I heard this story and my heart ached. I felt like her story was my own.

If I had returned to my parents, who always fought because of me, I would have been like the friend of my friend. I would have locked myself in a house and then given up on myself and my child. It takes courage to give birth to a baby and send the baby away. I realized that I could bring up my child but it wasn't because I was better than other people or because I had confidence in myself.

I will be more honest. When I think to myself honestly and calmly, I come to realize the profound reason that I chose to keep my baby: I feared that nobody would love me. I needed someone who would love me unconditionally. That was the reason I chose to bring up my baby rather than give her up for adoption. When I realized that, I felt so ashamed, and felt sorry for other mothers who had chosen adoption. I cried all day long. I was so lucky that so many hands had helped me.

So at the university I really did my best to get many certificates and good grades. Sometimes my heart ached and I felt sorry for my child because I couldn't spend enough time with her even though she was the reason I worked so hard. I studied harder to compensate for my lack of time with my child. I graduated and applied for jobs at some companies, but did not succeed. I had many certificates, good grades, and recommendation letters from the professors of my university. Even though I passed written exams and interviews, I failed the final steps. When I found out the reason I failed was that I was an unwed single mother, I got so discouraged.

One day one of my professors advised me not to tell the interviewers that I am an unwed single mother, that it would be okay to tell them after I got hired. I followed that advice and I was able to join one company immediately. I worked twice as hard as other colleagues so I could get credit and recognition. My boss and coworkers acknowledged my ability. And then I told them the truth that I was an unwed single mother. Everyone was surprised but soon understood. Some colleagues encouraged me. So now I am working for quite a big company as a designer. I do my best every day in working and in bringing up my child. My family opened their hearts and accepted my child and me as they saw me doing well. I was really happy. Everyone who accepted my child and me has helped me and my family. I'm living a worthwhile life because they're beside me. I am especially thankful to supporters of Ae Ran Won. Without them I would not have had a chance to get job training and to go to a university and so I would not be able to live like I live now.

I understand, as I learned at Ae Ran Won, that "both adoption and raising a child are the same difficult things . . . Thinking in a right and broad way for the value of life . . . Those two choices all deserve to get blessed by everyone in the world."

If someone chooses adoption, it could be the only option left to her, or it could be a mistake made by an immature woman. Maybe she is too young to know what she is doing. But in either case, mothers who bravely give birth alone deserve applause.

I have one last thing I really want to tell you: Whether you are an adoptee or have been brought up by your own mother who gave birth to you, you have the chance of life thanks to your mother's deep love.

 ### A note from Sangsoon Han

Miss Lee was a very sincere and thoughtful woman. She was tall and in good shape. When she first came to Ae Ran Won she seemed unable to face the fact that she was a pregnant. But through counseling, she realized that she needed to accept the truth to become a good mother.

When Ae Ran Seumter was established in 2001, it was run as an integrated program with Ae Ran Won. The purpose of Ae Ran Won is to help young birth mothers be independent after giving up their babies for adoption. Ae Ran Seumter is a mothers and babies' home to help single mothers who decide to raise their babies.

At Ae Ran Seumter, Miss Lee used to scold other young single mothers who did not manage their lives well. She told them that if the program's supporters knew this, they would not want to help them anymore. This made it difficult for her to develop good relationships with them. But soon she found out that they had been abused by their parents, and with love in her heart, she began to understand them. And she set a good example as a hard working student and was a role model for young single mothers.

After she was told that Ae Ran Won provided a scholarship she went to a university. She studied really hard there so she could win a department scholarship that was awarded to only one student in each department. When she won the department scholarship she became worried. She thought that if she told Ae Ran Won that she won the scholarship she would have to give the Ae Ran Won scholarship money back. But she wanted to spend the Ae Ran Won money to help her child and herself. After thinking about it for a while she decided to tell Ae Ran Won about everything. Above all she chose to live an honest life.

I was thankful to her in two ways. First, she studied hard and did her best even though she faced the difficult circumstances of bringing up her baby and earning a living. Second, she was brave enough to be honest. I let her use the money as she wanted because Ae Ran Won had already given her the scholarship. She was so happy for that. And she kept being awarded the scholarship in her university department.

She told me that at first her goal was to just make a living with her child. But her new goal is to work in the fashion industry in Milan, Italy. I was so proud of her. She is now a clothing designer. Before, she got help from other people, but now she saves money and gives help to neighbors in need. And she comes to the group counseling sessions and workshops of Ae Ran Won and tells her stories. This helps single mothers make good decisions about their babies' futures.

Miss Lee got many awards in design contests. Her talent is recognized and she was very active in work. But one morning she felt a bad pain in her back and chest and was sent to an emergency room.

Her illness was diagnosed as an exfoliation of the main artery and she was hospitalized in an intensive care unit. The factor of that disease was fatigue but the profound factor was Marfan Syndrome, which is an incurable genetic disease. Marfan Syndrome is a very rare disease that develops in one's thirties. Its symptoms affect the spine and vision as well as the main artery, which gets weaker and weaker.

Fortunately she got better, but she was told that she can never overextend herself, so she quit her job. She then made her living by making clothes and selling them on the Internet. She also repaired clothes. Her daughter was happy because she had more time with her mom, so Miss Lee was thankful.

After that, she got treatment at Hyundae Asan Hospital, which has Marfan Syndrome specialists. One day she was advised that she had to have surgery to save her life. Her vein was contracting. Her doctor said if she did not have the surgery, her vein would explode and she could die. The surgery cost 1.2 million won, and would take twelve hours. She decided to have the surgery. It was for her daughter rather than for herself. Ae Ran Won was called to discuss the situation with the hospital's social work team. As a result, Ae Ran Won introduced Miss Lee to the Korean Heart Fund and she received five million won from the fund. The hospital also gave her a discount. But the surgery does not guarantee a perfect cure, and she may need another surgery in the future. For now, Miss Lee is recovering, and at the time of this writing in 2009 she has had no further signs of the disease, but she worries about her daughter's future because she will likely have to go through another surgery.

$\mathscr{T}$ry Hard to Live a Happy Life

(baby born in 2002)

I would like to introduce myself. I am a healthy woman, five foot four inches tall and a hundred and twenty-three pounds, with fair skin. I wear glasses. I like to wear my dark brown hair short and straight. I am introverted and likely to cry or show my temper when angered. My family consists of my parents, my younger sister, and me. My family members are all Catholic. My parents are diligent and decent and of the philosophy that you receive only as much as you give. They don't have any sons, but believe that there is nothing women cannot do. My father is warm, responsible, and keeps regular hours, so much so that he is sometimes like a clock. My mother is energetic. When she reads a book, she occasionally underlines words that she wants to keep in mind or writes them down in a notebook. I have picked up this habit from her.

I used to like reading very much and when I was young my favorite gifts were books. I enjoyed telling my mother the stories I had read in books. When I was in fifth grade, my mom bought me a series of books. At first, I focused on reading them instead of sleeping. My parents wanted me to keep a written record of how I spent the pocket money they gave me, and they would check it each month. They participated in a parents association at my school unless they were too busy. My parents showed great interest in my life because I am their firstborn.

I didn't have many friends because of my introverted nature. I preferred to have deep relationships with just a few friends. I would become more cheerful and talkative when I got close to someone. I had been quiet throughout my whole school life. Whenever I had to speak up in class, my face always turned red and my voice got small. My dream? When I was in elementary school I wanted to be a teacher. During middle school I wanted to be a businessperson. I am good at making things with my hands. I spent my youth riding my bicycle, doodling, playing pool, inline skating, folding paper, and listening to music, especially Bach and cello compositions.

After graduating from college, I received computer training at an institute. I made friends with the tutors and one of them became the father of my baby. He and I got close, fell in love, and then had a relationship for one year. I recall that it was about a year into seeing each other when we slept together for the first time. It developed quite naturally as we loved each other, but I think that getting pregnant was my fault.

We had sex three days after my period. I was worried about getting pregnant but stopped thinking about it after a while. Surprisingly, I felt my periods getting shorter and shorter, and my ovulation cycle seemed irregular. When I noticed the first signs of pregnancy, I didn't feel sorry so much as nervous. I didn't know how to deal with this situation and I never imagined that I would experience something like it. I was afraid of telling my parents and friends. I assumed that people who knew me well might condemn me for having a baby without being married. I was more concerned with the social stigma of the situation than with the welfare of my baby.

I told my boyfriend that I might be pregnant, so we went to a hospital together to check it out. They allowed me to hear the sound of the baby's heartbeat. I couldn't believe that a baby was growing in my body, and didn't catch what the doctor was saying because I was so shook up. After leaving the hospital, I felt like fainting over the fact that I was pregnant. My boyfriend suggested that we get married. I really appreciated his offer but didn't have much faith in it since he had quit his job and was experiencing economic difficulties.

I went to my sister's house, in Seoul, because I was worried that my parents might notice my pregnancy. My sister knew that I was pregnant and she looked after me very well by buying nutritious foods and snacks. I felt ashamed that I wasn't a good role model for her as her older sister, but she only focused on my well-being. I am grateful to my sister because I cannot imagine how I would have managed without her. Twenty days after leaving home, my mother asked me to come back and I had no choice but to do so. That day, while I was doing the dishes after dinner, my mother called me into her room. She said my belly looked strange, and touched it, then said that I seemed pregnant. Finally, she asked me if I was, and I had to answer honestly. Yes.

That same night, my parents invited my boyfriend over. They said that he and I should get married. I thought that they would scold me, but they only cried because they thought I would be poor. I felt so badly. They were disappointed that I hadn't confided in them—they had always encouraged me to talk to them if I was in trouble. My parents are really good parents, but I'm not a good daughter. I have no idea why I am this way, especially when my sister is so decent. I hated myself for causing my parents anguish. After everything was out in the open, though, I felt light and free. Most of all, I was satisfied that I didn't have to go around trying to hide my burgeoning belly. I ate what I felt like and was really happy, but that didn't last long. Everyday, I prayed for my boyfriend's economic situation to improve. As my belly kept getting bigger, I became uncomfortable being at home—I didn't want my parents to feel ashamed if people noticed that I was pregnant.

At the time, I remembered hearing something on TV about a facility for unmarried women. It was selfish of me to think only about myself, so I called directory assistance and was introduced to Ae Ran Won. My parents gave me

permission to enter, but I was worried about staying there.
I had never experienced group living before, and I was
afraid that my reserved nature would make life difficult for
me. I was also nervous about living with others in the same
situation as mine. But even though I knew that it would be
hard, I didn't want to cause my parents any more grief.
I just appreciated having a place to go to. I got used to
being in Ae Ran Won after just two weeks. It no longer
seemed odd to see so many women with big bellies, but
sometimes I would get really irritated. Living with many
different kinds of people was not easy for me, but it was
comforting that we all had one thing in common.

There were many programs at Ae Ran Won and I especially
enjoyed attending the class in flower arranging. I felt good
about being able to look at flowers in my room after
finishing the class. I also attended a computer class to learn
word processing and spreadsheet skills. I liked this course
because I also gained social skills from it. While doing
prenatal exercises, I was able to overcome my fear of
childbirth. It was a pleasure to talk to the doctors and
nurses while taking walks during the day and at night.
I felt refreshed even though my legs got sore after walking.

I could see my situation clearly through the group
discussions that helped us to decide about our babies'
futures. At that point, my boyfriend said he couldn't marry
me because of his complicated family situation. However,
he didn't tell me what the issue was. I was frustrated
because I couldn't bring up my baby without a father. I
think that a father and mother should bring up their baby

together. Unless children have both parents, other children might look down on them when they go to school. In addition, people might talk about me behind my back if they know that I am a single mother, and my child might suffer for it.

Were it not for being in this situation, I might not be so distrustful of society. Since I feared the consequences of keeping the baby, I thought that giving him up for adoption might be better. Of course, I might be wrong for not considering what my baby would want. If my baby had been able to tell me that he wanted me to raise him despite the difficulties, I wouldn't have given him up.

To tell you the truth, I considered more than just my baby's needs when I made the decision to put him up for adoption. I was also worried about losing social standing if my situation was found out, and I was afraid that I would not be able to handle the consequences. I was worried about my parents, too. They were born, raised, and married in the same town their whole lives, but how could they walk down the street if people knew my secret? I felt so ashamed that I didn't want to live anymore. I thought it would be better to be dead. My parents actually wanted me to put the baby up for adoption, even though they didn't say it directly.

In Korea, adopted children have difficulties living in a society that discriminates against them. Therefore, it would be better for my baby to grow up in a developed country with a good educational system. If my baby is adopted overseas, I can contact him when he becomes an adult and hear news about him occasionally. However, that can almost never happen in Korea, so I wanted to send my baby abroad. On the other hand, despite the multiethnic makeup of the United States, I was worried that my baby might be discriminated against because of his skin color. Still, I was more worried about the prejudice in Korean society against adopted children, as well as unwed mothers, in case the domestic adoption is revealed. Then again, no matter where he lives, I wouldn't know how he's doing because I wouldn't be with him. I just have to believe that my baby will have a good life. If I think positively, everything will be okay, right?

After I gave birth at the hospital, my mother came to Ae Ran Won and helped me. She brought baby clothes and took care of the baby. I regret that my baby left wearing it, because if I had kept the clothing, I would have still been able to smell him. I miss my little boy. I want to feel his tiny hands and feet and smell his scent again. After he came out, a nurse put him on my chest and I kissed his hand. He was crying at the time. I can remember it vividly. Maybe, I can never forget. My mother felt sorry because I am her first child and my baby is her first grandchild. However, she told me that I should give up my baby because I was more important. My mother was with me while I gave birth, telling me how precious it was to bring life into the world. She cried because she didn't know how hard it would be to give him away. I think my mother also wants to see my baby again but my father doesn't miss him the way my mother does. It might still be hard for him, I guess. When I sent my baby away, I hoped the Virgin Mary would keep him. It was hard to let him go.

I regret that I didn't talk to him more. He should have heard my voice a lot before leaving me. I should have cared for him by reading books, thinking positively, and listening to music before he was born. Instead, I just felt angry. I know that it is useless to feel regret about it now, but I can't help it. I am worried that my depression might have affected the baby's character. I'm sure he must have had a tough time being inside my body. When I entered Ae Ran Won, I hoped that my boyfriend would resolve his financial problem and that we would be able to live together with our baby. My boyfriend wouldn't talk about him, and could only apologize. That is why I had such a depressing time. I knew that I shouldn't have been so pessimistic for the baby's sake but I couldn't control my feelings.

After I made the decision to give him up, I didn't want to hear the sound of a baby's cry at Ae Ran Won. Whenever I heard a baby crying, I felt like my baby was crying. I was very envious of the other mothers at Ae Ran Won because, unlike me, they were brave enough to bring up their baby themselves. One of the other residents said that pregnancy was the only peaceful time for her during her stay. I finally realized what she meant—the only time my baby and I could be together was when he was inside me. After giving birth, I felt depressed and empty. I was very sad not to feel my baby's presence anymore. Sometimes, I touched my belly and remembered what it felt like when he used to be in there. When it got warmer, I would go for a walk and encounter toddlers waddling along with scarves around their necks. Whenever I see a baby boy, I want to hold him and touch him because he reminds me of my baby. I hold back, though, because his parents might think me insane if I did that.

One day, a person in charge at the adoption agency came to me and asked me to sign an adoption agreement and give a written promise to give up my parental rights. It felt horrible to do it. I almost panicked because I was so afraid of what I was doing. Give up my parental rights? I was stunned that the concept even existed. Adoption turned into reality when I faced the adoption papers. It felt strange that my baby was no longer going to be mine. No one can understand what that feels like unless they have experienced it themselves. I had visited a Catholic priest so that my baby could be baptized before he was adopted. When I made the request after telling my story, the priest refused it on the grounds that I was not Catholic myself, even though my family was. I knew the real reason was because I was an unwed mother, but I was hoping that my son would still be able to receive this blessing from God. It was upsetting that I couldn't get this for my baby.

I am thinking a lot about my baby's adoptive parents, wondering who they are. I hope they are parents who are able to love, cherish, and sometimes scold my son in a loving way. I hope they travel on vacations with their children and participate in a parents association. Why? Because that's the kind of parent I want to be. If there's anything that I could wish for, it is that my son would be healthy and cheerful. Even though he might realize he is adopted, I want him to grow up without feeling sad or desperate. Actually, I want to meet him as a healthy, well-raised boy or young man someday.

If I were to meet him, what would I say? I think I would touch his face, hands, feet and ears, put his hands on my face and listen for his heart beat, and finally I would hold him for a long time. I hope I don't die of surprise when I meet him. I will ask if he had kept the ring that I gave him before he was adopted. If I meet my child after he becomes an adult, I want to show him the dress that I wore when I was pregnant, pictures of us together before he was adopted, and all his baby things. I also want to take him to the hospital where I gave birth and meet with the doctor who delivered him and show him the room that I stayed in. Finally, we would visit Ae Ran Won and see what my life was like there. I want to show my son everything that he wants to remember or know. Is it possible?

Blessed Mary, help me. I frequently feel sad since my baby left. I feel a lot of guilt. Everything was my fault from the beginning. His birth should have been acknowledged and celebrated by others. I created unhappy circumstances for my baby. Therefore, I will never forgive myself for being so irresponsible and thoughtless. I don't know how to deal with the pain of missing him. I am having such a tough time recovering. Will a day ever come when every little boy on the street won't remind me of him? I don't think so. I think it will still hurt if I see little boys the same age as my son, who will be two years old next year. I think I will feel guilt for the rest of my life since I don't know how to overcome it. However, I have a responsibility to behave like a proud mother when my son comes to see me.

To keep myself occupied, I began learning how to cook. This is something that I like to do. I want to open my own restaurant in two or three years. Of course, I should work hard as well as experience other things. My mind still wanders, but I am trying to move forward for the future. I hope that I can persist without giving up, and I hope I can show my son how successful I am. My situation has improved a lot since last year. I had felt gloomy being at home without doing anything, so I tried to find something that I was interested in and could learn about. I became certified in Western cooking, confectionary, and baking. I trained hard from morning to night. Now I am preparing for another test.

The biggest change for me is that I got married to a guy my parents introduced me to. I told him about my past before we started dating. Then we talked about marriage, and he told his parents about my experience. When he told me that he had talked about me to his parents, I was embarrassed. However, I think it might be better this way, because I won't have to feel nervous about having something to hide anymore. My husband is a public official who is sincere and considerate. He would never hurt me and I really appreciate him. I still think about my son and feel sad but I pray for him whenever I feel like that. I want to live happily ever after and hope that my son does, too. I want to meet him someday and will try hard to live a happy life.

A note from Sangsoon Han

This mother stays in touch with Ae Ran Won and has become a good supporter. Each Christmas season she comes to Ae Ran Won with cakes she baked herself. She purposely bakes them plain, and has a contest among the birth mothers at Ae Ran Won for who can do the best decoration of a cake. It's a fun event that is perfect for the holiday season.

$\mathcal{S}$triving for Independence

(baby born in 2002)

I really don't know much about my family. I never heard anything about them because I was abandoned at the age of three and grew up in an orphanage until I was eighteen. Unfortunately, I know nothing of what kind of parents I was born from, if I have any siblings, or why I was discarded on the street. What I remember from my childhood is being surrounded by heaps of kids my age, because I grew up in an orphanage.

When I think back to my school days, only an empty smile crosses my face. I recall puberty starting around eighth grade for me. Even the adults had a hard time handling me since I was so headstrong and stubborn. People started to treat me as a troublemaker. They did their best to stay far away from me, making sure they had nothing to do with me. My school days were truly depressing and hard to bear.

Perhaps for these reasons, for as far back as I can remember, I never had any dreams. I lived each day as it passed by. Of course, I had vague desires to become something. I remember wanting to become a scientist in junior high, and a musician or lead singer of a rock band during high school.

Since I stirred up a lot of trouble at school and the orphanage, getting my high school diploma was very hard. As soon as I graduated, I had to leave the orphanage. I found a monthly rental and cooked meals for myself while making ends meet with a part-time job at a video game room. For the first time, I realized that I was truly alone in this world. And I was very lonely. There was a guy who frequented the game room around then, and he was kind to me. I was so overwhelmed by loneliness at the time that his display of interest prompted me to start dating him. In a short period of time, we became very close. He demanded sex from me, and I was unable to refuse his request. Soon after my first sexual experience, I found out that I was pregnant. It was my first relationship and first pregnancy, and I was shocked that I got pregnant after my first sexual experience. I wanted to tell him about the pregnancy. But before I could, he told me he was going to study abroad and then immediately left—I never even got a chance to tell him that I was pregnant. Just like that, our short relationship came to an abrupt end. I was completely alone again.

Being pregnant took its toll on my body but I had good feelings toward the baby. Knowing that I wasn't "alone" in the world, and that even I had a blood relation, gave me great consolation. At first I tried to hide my pregnancy, but before long people around me started to notice. My friends and elders from the orphanage seemed to take the news calmly, but I could sense that the nuns were quite upset. They were uncomfortable even with my visits to the orphanage because they thought I would set a bad example for the other children there.

I was living in Busan when I found out about my pregnancy, and out of distress, I just went back to my orphanage in Seoul without any definite plans. (This orphanage has a school facility for elementary school students in Seoul and junior high school and high school facilities in Busan. When kids graduate from elementary school, they're moved to Busan and stay at that facility.)

At the time of my pregnancy, I had nothing in my possession. I was in desperate need of help. So to get help, I hastily rushed to Seoul and met with the nun who raised me from a young age and told her the truth about what happened. I stayed at the orphanage for about two months and the nun told me about Ae Ran Won, a pregnancy center that helped unmarried mothers with childbirth. This was how I was admitted to Ae Ran Won.

Before going to Ae Ran Won, it was hard dealing with the changes I was going through because there weren't any single mothers around me at all. But going to Ae Ran Won changed everything. Knowing that I wasn't the only person like this was a huge comfort and relief. I was already used to life in facilities, so adjusting to group life wasn't tough for me. Instead, living with people who shared the same problems I had gave me the opportunity to get close to them easily. There were a lot of things I craved to eat after getting pregnant and there was no need to worry about this either—the pregnancy center provided everything I needed. Soon, I gave birth and decided to give my child up for adoption. Of course, I wanted to raise my child myself more than anything. My baby was the only blood relation I had in this world, so why wouldn't I want to keep the baby close by my side? Even so, I chose adoption without hesitation.

It's hard to clearly articulate the reason I chose adoption, but what anchored my decision was a strong desire to make sure my child did not grow up without parents like I did. I couldn't bear to have the child grow up lonely and weary, navigating the world alone. More than anyone, I knew how miserable and painful that could be.

No matter how much I wanted to, there was nothing I could do for the child at that time. That was why I chose adoption. I attended group counseling where we discussed the future of our children but, from the beginning, I felt like I didn't even have a choice. When the nuns at my orphanage heard of my decision for adoption, they told me that I did the right thing.

After deciding on adoption, I felt pathetic about myself. It was because I kept thinking that I would've raised my child alone if only I had the capacity and means to do so. I felt pity for myself—that I had to send off my one and only blood-relation—and my baby. I'm just so sorry to my child.

As I send my child away for adoption, what I expect from the adoptive parents is that they will love and shelter my baby, just as they would with a baby born between them. Also, I hope they will listen closely to the things my baby says. What I hope for my child is that he grows up to become a positive person, in thoughts and actions. To achieve what he really wants to do in life and, even when things get tough in life, to persevere and continue to grow as a decent human being.

There is no way I could describe what I felt after sending my child off. Every time my child's birthday draws near, I'm filled with this inexpressible variety of complex and profound feelings and go through an agonizing psychological struggle. At those times, I couldn't do anything, and just sat with a vacant stare. After arriving at Seumter, I celebrated my baby's hundred-day ceremony and first birthday with my Seumter family. We bought a cake and lit the candle and sat around together, wishing for my baby's happiness. I believe that was all I did, because that was all I could do.

I just prayed that my baby, whom I loved dearly, would be surrounded by the kind of loving family I never had. Having a wonderful birthday party—with presents from brothers, sisters, and parents—all singing together and having a great time, as a family.

At that time, I was agonizing over a worry that besieged me. In the near future, I'd have to leave Ae Ran Won and I was anxious because I had nowhere to go. I dreaded going back to the convent orphanage and, since I was past my teens, it was also a place that could no longer accept me.

After giving birth, there was nowhere I could go and the future seemed so bleak when I thought about it. What I liked most about Ae Ran Won was that it guided me during this time so that even a hopeless case like me could harbor hope. It also made me realize that there was a way to achieve such hope. It was by entering Seumter. I knew that there was a group home called Ae Ran Seumter run by Ae Ran Won to help prepare mothers in gaining independence, but I never thought I would be fortunate enough to join the family there. It was because I always thought that luck and good fortune were out of my reach.

During a counseling session with an assigned social welfare social worker, I was introduced to Seumter and given an opportunity to join the center. Ae Ran Seumter is a place where single mothers prepare to gain independence. It was where one must have plans and motivation about the future, but I had neither plans nor the will power at that time.

During my counseling sessions, though, I came to discover one goal. It was to become a dog groomer. Ever since I was little, I liked dogs a lot. It could be because I didn't have any close friends. The dog at the orphanage was my only true friend. If I'd see a dog while walking along the street, I'd be drawn and end up petting it. And many times I'd been bitten, but that didn't stop me from liking dogs. It was easy for me to decide on becoming a dog groomer as my goal. My social worker assigned me homework: to research twenty different breeds of dogs through the Internet or books. When I returned soon after with the completed assignment, my social worker was happy for me and said it seemed like I was really into dogs, and that if I did something I truly loved, I would eventually excel at it.

After settling down at Ae Ran Seumter, I started attending a dog grooming school and ultimately obtained a level 3 and level 2 dog grooming certificate.

I was thrilled that I could receive help and support for something I wanted to do. At the orphanage, I was never given the opportunity to learn about something I wanted to do. No one there had ever asked me what I wanted to do in the future. Through learning and hard work, I've become a competent dog groomer. I am so grateful for this opportunity, which allowed me to become psychologically and financially stable and to grow as an independent individual.

I am currently in a relationship and will soon be married. Even after marriage, I plan to continue to work in the dog grooming industry, and I hope to have children. I truly want to become an understanding and attentive mother. The most meaningful thing to me is to have a family of my own.

A note from Sangsoon Han

This young woman married soon after writing this piece and gave birth to a pretty daughter. After having such an unhappy life while in the orphanage, she has found the life she dreamed of. She is living a happy life with the family that she had hoped, all her life, to join and create.

chapter 15

Change Begins with Me

(baby born in 2003)

I come from a family of five—my parents, two sisters, and me. My father, a man of few words, was very strict with us. We were not allowed to have our ears pierced, our hair dyed, or to stay out late. Going against his rules would lead to a terrifying beating. For that reason, I was always afraid of Dad, and it caused me to go astray. My mother was always at my side with a bright smile on her face. However, being dependent upon Dad, she could not protect us from him. I think I took after some of her bright personality. My sisters are three and seven years younger than me. Because of our very different personalities, we would often get into conflicts, but I'm proud to say that we still manage to be very close to each other. Since I was the firstborn child and was always afraid of, and hated, my father, I was desperate to become independent. (Now, my dad is a very caring, responsible, and exemplary father.)

When I was young, I had little confidence and was very shy. But as I went to middle school and made friends, my personality changed. I started to rebel and talk back to my father for no reason. I started smoking and drinking. Being short and kind of chubby made me self-conscious and distanced me from people.

During my first year of high school, my friends set me up with a boy. Meeting someone who liked me opened my eyes to the opposite sex. But I was fed up with my home life, so I attempted many times to run away, and eventually I quit high school. After my first ride in that boy's car, I enjoyed riding in a lot of cars. I met many people this way, including a very young and naïve boy, who would be the father of my child. I let go of most of my relationships, except for a few close friends, and saw only him during the summer that I was sixteen.

I was a teenage runaway doing nothing. I relied on my boyfriend for support and naturally his parents found out about me. With my boyfriend's encouragement, little by little I felt secure enough to go back home. With no skills or education, I had to get a job at a factory. At that point, I didn't have any dreams of my own. Two years passed by. My boyfriend and I got into a lot of fights but still loved each other enough to see each other pretty much every day. I still believe that he had true feelings towards me then.

Naturally, we had sex together until I found out I was pregnant in the springtime of my eighteenth year.

I immediately told my boyfriend the news and he wanted to have the baby. Back then he was only a senior in high school and had no economic means. I knew that his parents disapproved of me seeing him, so when he said that he would like to have the baby, it didn't seem realistic. I thought it would be impossible for us to raise a child and convinced him to let me have an abortion.

At the time, I didn't know how dangerous it would be to have repeated abortions. I regret putting myself in that position. Six months after getting the abortion, I got pregnant again and had to have another abortion. After the second time, I realized that I was damaging my health. Rather than learning from the effects of reckless sexual behavior, we decided that the next time I got pregnant we would tell our parents and get permission to raise the child. During those three years I spent with my boyfriend, I thought he would think of and love only me.

After a while, I realized we were drifting apart. We would get into a lot of fights because he would either see other girls or spend time without me. One day, out of frustration, I blurted out "Let's break up!" He responded as if he had been waiting for these words and agreed to the break up. A week had passed when I realized how dependent I had become on him, so I lied about being pregnant, knowing that he always wanted children.

So he came back to me and for a short moment I was happy again. As he showed me more attention, I had to lie more, and that made me very nervous. As we reached a point where I thought our relationship had recovered, I lied and told him I had had another abortion. Saying that he could not forgive me, he left me. I felt so guilty that I couldn't stop him. A week had passed, and finding it strange that my period hadn't come, I got a pregnancy test and it came out positive, two very clear purple lines. I had no clue what to do. I ran away from home and stayed at a friend's house and sent my boyfriend a text message saying that I was pregnant. He responded with, "Aren't we officially over?" so I decided not to use this baby to get back together with him.

Three months passed when I realized that my friend was not comfortable with me staying there, so I had to find a place to stay with my baby. Through an Internet search for facilities for unwed mothers, I found my way to Ae Ran Won.

After being admitted to the facility, the social worker knew it would be difficult for me to raise the child alone and recommended that I consider adoption. There was a group meeting concerning the baby's future where we had to discuss what resources we had to raise the child. I had no resources and no one to help me. I didn't see any other options, and thought it was best for the child. I tried to contact the father again and was disappointed again.

Although I had already decided to give my child up for adoption, I wanted to check my boyfriend's reaction one last time by letting him know how much I wanted to raise this child and that I still had feelings for him. I must not have expressed myself well because his reaction was very negative. I cried and cried. I cried to the point that I knew was hurting the baby. I stopped crying and promised the baby, "Although I can't take care of you to the end, for the time you are in me, I will give you happiness."

I gradually got used to life at Ae Ran Won. Most of all, I was really grateful to the social workers who helped me participate in the cultural activities and educational programs for the baby. I also started receiving counseling from the adoption agency. After a lot of counseling, I had to decide which option was better for the child—domestic or overseas adoption. After agonizing for a while, I decided to go for domestic adoption, but the social workers at the adoption agency explained that if they couldn't find adoptive parents in Korea, the child would have to be sent abroad. The clock was ticking toward the delivery date. With a month to go, I found out that Ha Eun (the name I gave to my child) was upside down, and a C-section was scheduled.

Until then, my parents didn't know I was pregnant. On the day before the operation, I called my mom and told her of my pregnancy. Because I was a minor, the hospital needed the approval of a guardian. I really wanted Ae Ran Won to sign the papers instead but Ae Ran Won could not act as my legal guardian. So I had no other choice than to ask my mother to approve the operation.

I couldn't bear to tell my mother that I was pregnant and needed surgery, so I had the social worker call her up for me. I didn't have the heart to talk to my mother on the phone, but after she heard the news she insisted on talking to me and I had no other choice. She only asked, "Is your stomach big?" and I burst into tears. The next day, my mother came to the hospital and signed the papers for me. I had the surgery and gave birth to Ha Eun.

There is no better word than "lovely" to describe my baby. My lovely baby—she seemed so docile. The next day, before I could even understand all the emotions I was feeling, the hospital took Ha Eun away. It felt like my baby was being stolen from me and I cried for a long time. After the baby was gone, like most mothers in this situation, I went through a very hard time. No matter where I went or who was there, I couldn't stop crying. I couldn't stop thinking about the baby and being tortured by guilt and regret. When things were bothering me, my baby was the reason to keep on going, but afterward, when I was in pain and confusion, nothing could make me feel better. I could never forgive myself for irresponsibly having a child and sending it away. I just wanted to end my life.

After spending some time feeling lost, I imagined that one day, my child, all grown up, would come looking for me, and I thought I could never meet my child living like this. The TV programs in which adult adoptees look for their birth parents also came to my mind. I also thought about experiences I had with adult adoptees in a group meeting. I could not face my child if I didn't make myself better.

Something had to change, so I began to think about my future.

As I thought about my future, I got interested in the high school qualification exam and job training program. The social worker informed me of an opening at Ae Ran Seumter and persuaded me to enroll. I already knew that Ae Ran Seumter was a facility run by Ae Ran Won for teenagers who gave up their children for adoption, but I didn't think it had anything to do with me. Now that I found the motivation to live, I had to change my image, so I decided to enroll in Ae Ran Seumter.

Even after I enrolled, despite my intentions, the sorrow and guilt about my child took over, and for some time I could do nothing. I gradually came back to my senses, thinking that this could be my last chance to use my life to the fullest. Drawing upon all my willpower, I registered at an institute and went daily to study for the high school qualification exam. I even studied when I got back home. Seumter connected us with volunteer teachers to whom we could ask questions about what we learned and who guided us through our studies. I studied really hard and earned a high school diploma. Then I completed a one-year course to become a specialist in skin care and hair design. I also took up a job that the institute introduced me to. Through the two years I stayed at Seumter, I achieved everything I wanted.

I didn't have high expectations of myself but I achieved my goals. I couldn't believe it. The most important lesson I gained out of staying at Seumter was learning to get along with the people around me. People of all different personalities and ages gave birth and had to give up their children for adoption. Because of our common scar, we had to get along with people who weren't our family, and it wasn't easy. In the past, I found it difficult to be with other people and, due to my insecurities, preferred to be alone. Now, however, I get along with others.

When my two years at Seumter were almost over, the social worker set up several talks with my father. The social worker also conducted communication training and child-education classes. This was done so that I could feel safe when I went back to my home. Our family learned a lot concerning family interactions, and my relationship with my father was resolved.

Today, I am working hard as a skin care specialist at a well-known shop in the Gangnam area of Seoul. At first, learning the ropes was not as easy as I had expected, and I changed jobs. I worked hard, my salary went up, and now I am very satisfied with my job. Whenever I get a chance, I try to learn from my coworkers. I need to learn more about my field, and to do that I plan to go to a technical college. I am now twenty-three years old. When I first arrived at Ae Ran Won, I was a foolish eighteen-year-old. Looking back, I see that I have matured in many respects. I am also more confident and financially independent. I am very proud of myself for having been able to make such changes.

I believe that rather than waiting for Korean society to change, I must change first, before I can ask the world to accept me. This is something I learned late. Although the people at Ae Ran Won and Seumter and I don't come from the same blood, they are a family that I love and they have helped me to become mature. I wish I'd met them earlier instead of having wasted my time.

I am not concerned about what kind of parents Ha Eun is being raised by. I only wish for her to be healthy and happy with them. I don't know what kind of parents can do that. I believe one day my child will come and look for me. I will stay in contact with the adoption agency so that when my child comes for me, I will be easy to find.

They say I can't look for my child until she turns eighteen, so I will wait. When my child finds me, I will explain why I could not be with her. I want to express the emotions that I kept inside and say, "I love you." I might then ask if she loves me or hates me or feels the same way as I do.

 A note from Sangsoon Han

After she left Ae Ran Won, this birth mother kept in touch with us, and was very happy to hear about this book project. She is anxious to have her story be in the book so that it can be read by adoptees. She is looking forward to hearing the reaction to the stories in this book when adoptees and adoptive families read it.

$\mathscr{H}$ealthy and Full of Humanity

(baby born in 2003)

I don't know how much this story will allow the many adoptees around the world to ease their suffering and to satisfy their desire to find their roots, but I wrote it with my deepest feelings in the hope that it might, in some small way, be of help.

Growing up under the care of the parents who conceived me, going to school and joining society, meeting a good person and starting my own family—what paradise could be more desirable than this? But sadly, I was never able to walk that completely normal path. Before I was even able to recognize my mother's face, my parents divorced, and I was sent to my maternal grandmother's house while our family register was rearranged. When I was three, I was separated from my mother when my father essentially kidnapped me.

Then, like we were going into hiding, he cut off all contact with my mother and got remarried after a year.

I was four. Because my father had remarried while I was so young, I grew up thinking that my stepmother was my real mother. The first few years, my new mother treated me as well as any mother would. When I started elementary school, we moved to Seoul because my stepmother needed to be closer to her own mother, to take care of her. My parents decided that one way they could help my new grandmother was to send me to her home to help with the housework. She lived in a neighborhood above ours, and had a small Buddhist shrine in her house. Strangely, whenever other Buddhists came to the house to pray and worship, she gave me some money and told me to play outside and not come into the house until they had left. The house was at the bottom of a mountain. In those days, we still used charcoal for heat, and if we needed hot water, we had to heat some up in a kettle. We couldn't just use it whenever we wanted, and after washing the dishes in winter, my frozen hands would swell up and crack.

Soon after, my younger brother was born, and to an oldest child who liked babies as much as I did, he was the prettiest thing I had ever seen. Every day after school, I would finish the chores at my grandmother's house and then run home to feed him milk, wash his diapers, rock him to sleep on my back when he got fussy at bedtime, and then go back up to Grandmother's. However, the birth of my brother changed my relationship with my stepmother. When I asked her if she was okay when she started having labor pains, she became furious. From that day on, she got angry at me over the smallest thing and would hit me with a switch until it broke. Eventually, she would hit me with her hand as soon as she saw me, and kick me out of the house all night. On those days my parents would argue, and their relationship became strained.

My father also had a violent temper, and when he scolded me he would hit me all over and try to kick me out. If I tried to stay in the house, he would throw pots, bricks, and rice bowls at me and then pick me up and throw me out. When I was young, I thought that I was lucky to get thrown out since I might have been killed otherwise. My father never paid attention to what I said. He always sided with my stepmother, and when he scolded me he would beat me into a stupor. It was inevitable that I started to close my mouth and my mind in front of my parents. I was shy and withdrawn, though, so I never rebelled against them or questioned them, even though they beat and scolded me. Instead, the more they yelled at me, the more I blamed myself for being ugly or somehow bad.

I learned the truth about my family in high school when my homeroom teacher, holding my family register, asked, "Did you know that your mother is really your stepmother?" But when I asked my father about it, he wouldn't tell me anything about my real mother, and I never let the topic pass my lips again. I thought that since I was almost an adult and she still hadn't tried to contact me, she must have forgotten about me, or maybe she had started another family and didn't feel comfortable contacting me. I stopped wondering about it and didn't think about looking for her.

I graduated from high school and wanted to continue on to college, but my father said he would be ashamed if I couldn't get into a top university. He said he couldn't give me any money and proceeded to rip up my textbooks. My stepmother, always troubled by money, constantly complained about me to my father, and since I also had two younger siblings, I felt pressure to earn money quickly. On top of that, if I did go to college, I would have to attend a public college, and even though I wanted to study design, I would have to major in telecommunications, which was cheap but offered a high employment rate. Angry at my parents and my terrible situation, I blindly sent out job applications. At that time, you could make the most money at banks and department stores. I got a job at a department store on the first try. Whether that was ultimately good or bad, I don't know.

So, even before I graduated, I started working at the department store. From then on, my dream was to make a lot of money and be recognized by my parents. It was really tough at first. Standing up nervously for more than ten hours straight was not easy. Still, happiness came into my otherwise gloomy life. When I got my first paycheck, my mother told me I had done a good job, and for the first time in a long while, I saw her smile. Seeing that made me so happy that, even though my legs felt like they would fall off and my supervisors constantly stressed me, I endured it patiently and worked hard.

Since I had to meet a lot of people in my job, and especially since I was a new employee, I had to attend a lot of after-work parties, so I came home late a lot of nights. My conservative father, however, believed it was unacceptable for a young woman to go out all the time. He eventually kicked me out of the house and kept my earnings, all the way from my first paycheck, leaving me penniless. If I had used my salary only on myself there would have been some left, but I had to give spending money to my parents and siblings and buy them snacks and clothes. You might say that I shouldn't have done that, and just kept the money for myself, but I had to spend money on them for them to take an interest in me. I enjoyed seeing their smiling faces so much that I ended up with a lot of credit-card debt.

Up to that point, I had never rebelled or said anything against my parents, but being kicked out penniless like that made me so angry that I told them to pay back all the money I had given them over the last four years. They told me to give back all the money they had spent on my food, clothing, and education while I was growing up. I was speechless. I wanted to run away somewhere and die. My parents, in their last reproach, said that they would kill me if they saw me again, and set the exact date and time for me to get out of the house. Eventually, I scraped together a little money and was able to rent a small room. With feelings of intense betrayal, depression, loneliness, and stress from work, I went through some difficult times.

A friend, saying that I needed cheering up, took me to a reunion of my elementary school classmates. It was there that I first met my son's father. I was a bit curious about him since he was quiet and attentive for his age, but I was very careful and serious about making friends with the opposite sex because my ideal was to be, as Koreans say, "a wise mother and a good wife." Not having been able to go to church or even the library due to my ultra-conservative upbringing, I was extremely cautious about associating with men if I didn't consider them to be potential husbands. However, my son's father appeared during a difficult and painful time in my life, and everything about him was so attractive that I soon became addicted to his presence, like a drug. I cautiously met him once, then twice. After that, our relationship gradually progressed until we moved in together.

I was sure that we would get married, so I did my best to please him. A year later, while I was preparing dinner as usual, I got a call from a woman. She said she was his girlfriend and asked who I was. At that instant, everything went white, and as I laughed dumbstruck, he came in the door with a confused look on his face. I had never even suspected that there was another woman, so I had no idea what to say. He explained that they had broken up after being together for four years, but he stayed in touch because she still had feelings for him. Since they had known each other so long, and it would be hard to suddenly cut off all contact with her, he asked me to give him one month to settle it. I hadn't had any relationship experience then, so I completely believed him and told him to do that. I even felt sorry for him since I figured it would be painful for him to leave someone he was so close to, and I tried even harder to make him comfortable.

One month passed, and since he hadn't said anything, I assumed that he had taken care of it. Several more months passed when I got another call from the same woman. This time, I went to meet her, and she told me the whole story. She said that he had never suggested that they stop meeting and instead had kept seeing her while lying to both of us. She said she was going to leave him, but I had invested too much love in the relationship to just give up. Also, I had already had an abortion with him, so I had to think hard before making a decision. He had always had a tough exterior, but when I confronted him, he started crying and said that he was sorry and that he couldn't live without me. I couldn't think logically, and the whole situation seemed like a crazy dream, so we stayed together.

He still continued to see her, and even though it hurt my pride, my stubbornness wouldn't let me quit. I allowed him to see her with the hope that, if I treated him well enough, he would eventually choose me. We spent two years like that. However, no matter how much I tried to understand, I couldn't forgive him in my heart, and we fought almost every day. We had never fought even once before, but because of that one sensitive issue we constantly shouted and got sick of each other. With all the stress in my life, my mind and body were exhausted.

During that time, I didn't use contraception, and I got pregnant again. When I had an abortion before, I felt guilty about it, but my son's father absolutely insisted on another abortion. I was sitting on a pile of debt, and I still really wanted to succeed on my own, so I felt like abortion was my only choice. He said he felt bad for me, but to him it was just an embryo, not a human, and he showed no remorse about it. I felt so ashamed of him. To try to settle things between the two of us and the other woman, and to give him some sense of responsibility, I waited to go to the hospital until I could think of what to do. Several months passed. I waited anxiously, but my son's father assumed that I would take care of the abortion myself and didn't talk about it.

Feeling that things couldn't go on like that, I borrowed money from a friend and went to the hospital for an ultrasound scan. I hadn't felt the baby move, so I thought it was still early in the pregnancy, but after the exam I found out that in another day or so I would be in my sixth month. When the doctor said it was too late for an abortion, I hadn't yet decided to raise the baby, but I still felt secretly happy. I had worried that the baby might be unhealthy since I couldn't feel it move, but at around ten o'clock that night, I felt something like a finger wiggling around inside. I was bursting with joy, but at the same time, I thought of how this little life inside of me had been so frightened that he hadn't even dared to move freely, and I sobbed with anguish. As the days passed, the baby started to move around more, and he started kicking and rolling around like crazy.

On the night I came back from the hospital, I told my son's father that it was too late for an abortion. I lied a little bit and said that even if I could find a hospital that would do it, it would cost an extreme amount of money and that I wouldn't be able to have children again. He went outside for about two hours. When he came back, the first thing he said, without any hesitation, was that I should send the baby away for adoption. He said that since he had no intention of breaking up with the other woman or taking care of this baby, I should put the baby up for adoption if I didn't want to screw up my future. I couldn't believe it. How could he make a decision like that after just two hours?

Honestly, I was angrier at him for saying that than I was when he said he wanted me to have an abortion. After hearing his irresponsible answer, I said I would raise the baby myself. He threatened to kill me. I was so angry with him that I went to meet his mother, but once again, I was a fool to expect any sympathy. She said that since she didn't know me, I should discuss the matter with her son. She also said that she would never accept my child as part of her family and told me not to expect anything from her. Then she left. I thought his parents would be different, but that hope was shattered to pieces; on the contrary, they thought I was using the baby to get money from them. When my son's father found out I had seen his mother, he cursed at me so cruelly that I wondered if he had ever loved me at all. But the more I suffered, the stronger my maternal instinct became, and I swore that even if I was going to give my baby up for adoption, I had to nurture it the best I could now.

Now I was always hungry, I couldn't work, and the baby's father wouldn't give me any money, so if I wanted to have the baby, I was going to have to go to a home for unmarried mothers. While I was having my regular checkup, I asked the hospital if they could help me, and that's how I heard about Ae Ran Won. Actually going there, however, was very difficult and scary. I thought that everyone in there would be emotionally hurt and wary like me, and I had little confidence that I, penniless and helpless, could adjust to living with them. But after a few days, people started to open their hearts to me, and the director and the kind social workers were like real mothers to me. They gave me nutritious snacks in case I wasn't getting enough to eat, and thanks to their thorough examinations, I felt secure and was able to concentrate on my prenatal education.

As the baby's movements became more frequent and the birth date got closer, the decision to keep the child or send it for adoption troubled me. Being a single mother in Korea is like being marked with a scarlet letter. In addition, my debt problems would make taking care of a child a huge burden. Still, just thinking about living without my child broke my heart, and I wasn't sure that sending him away would make me happy. On the other hand, my life would be more financially and emotionally stable if I put my child up for adoption, and I wondered if by keeping the baby I would be making his life more difficult just to satisfy my own selfishness.

In the end, I chose to put the baby up for adoption, and I swore to see him again someday. I selected an overseas adoption so that I would be able to stay in contact with the baby and help him not to feel like he had been abandoned. But I worried that, after going overseas, he might get sick and become a burden to his adoptive parents, and that they might feel less love for him, so I really wanted to breast-feed him with my first milk before sending him away. I thought that would be the most precious gift I could give him, so I made this request to Ae Ran Won. At first the director said that she understood how I felt, but my request would hurt the feelings of the adoptive mother and so was out of the question. I also understood how the other mother might feel, and that this was a difficult request, but I couldn't give up. Knowing that I would regret it for the rest of my life if I didn't, I asked her once again. This time, I got permission, and they agreed to give me eight days.

Finally, two weeks after the expected date, and after twelve hours of labor, I was blessed with a healthy baby boy. Looking at his calm face, I was able to experience true joy and emotion for the first time in my life. At the same time, I also felt sadness at the fact that I only had eight days left with him. After leaving the hospital, I lived with my son, but for the first five days I didn't produce any milk, so I wasn't able to breast-feed him as much as I wanted to before the eight days were up.

On the eighth day, I went to the adoption agency with his father. As soon as we arrived, the woman at the agency said that she had been waiting for a long time and quickly snatched my son away from me. The baby's father and I signed the release forms giving up our parental custody, and then we stood outside the door of the adoption agency. As I was coming down the stairs, my head was completely empty. My legs buckled, and I collapsed right there on the steps. At that moment, tears gushed up from the bottom of my heart and I couldn't hold them back. I don't think I've ever cried so hard in my life. After returning to Ae Ran Won, I couldn't function normally. When I woke up, my eyes were full of tears, and at night, my son would appear in my dreams, and I would feel sinful and couldn't sleep.

After a week of this half-dead existence, I decided that I couldn't go on that way and resolved to get my son back. Of course, I had no money, and piles of debt, but I thought that if only I had my son, I wouldn't be afraid of anything in the world. On the day that I got my son back, all the worries that had made me give him up disappeared, and I was full of confidence that I could take care of him so well that he would thank me when he was grown. I resolved to make a life for us that would be completely different from the week before. My heart was full of joy, and my happiness at having my own family made me thank God every day. However, as soon as I chose to raise my son, his father told me not to even think of contacting him, even if we were starving. My friends asked me why I was tying up my precious youth with raising a child. They told me that I should put him up for adoption again. But when I looked into my son's eyes and saw him try to talk, my fears about our life changed into confidence. At Ae Ran Won, I prepared step-by-step for our lives. First, I took an aptitude test and chose a career as a hairdresser. Then I got my certification and started a job search.

Without Ae Ran Won's help, I never would have been able to make these preparations or even dream of raising my son. Korean society still doesn't recognize the existence of single mothers, and without policies or support for us, it's extremely difficult for us to stand on our own. However, at the single mother's home at Ae Ran Won, and at my current single mother and child's home, I've been lucky and have been able to prepare for my future. Now my son is about thirty-two months old, and he hasn't gotten very sick or made me upset yet, so I'm so very thankful to him. Growing up without a father, I don't want him to feel hopeless and dejected; instead, I want him to be healthy, to be full of humanity, not just knowledge, and to be considerate to others. I think that in the future, because of the low birthrate, Korean society will also stop thinking badly of single mothers and will implement policies to help us. As for my dream, I hope to start a small beauty shop and make a living for me and my son.

In 2008, she opened her own beauty salon in Seoul. The money needed to start her salon came partly through Ae Ran Won, and also a social worker who helped the mother apply to a fund, by writing a proposal for her salon, and she was picked to get money from that fund. She has been leading a normal life with her son, who is now four years old. She has plans to emigrate to Australia, and is taking English lessons with a volunteer tutor every Wednesday at Ae Ran Won. She feels she and her son will have a brighter future in Australia, where she will have more opportunity in her career, and will be away from the social discrimination against her son that would be present in Korea.

$\mathcal{D}$reaming a World

(baby born in 2004)

A letter from the single mother of a birth mother:

"If it were just a dream . . . What could be more frightening or scary than this?" My mind went blank and I couldn't even breathe.

The tiny life that suddenly came to my daughter was not welcomed from the start. "My daughter is pregnant . . ." I could never believe it. It was far more shocking than a thunderbolt. Though I felt awfully sorry for the baby, my daughter's and my life meant more than anything else.

After I found out about my daughter's pregnancy, I hardly knew what to do. The first thing I had to do was hide my daughter, because I was afraid that other family members or some people we knew might notice. I was irritated, but I wasn't angry. Rather, I deeply pitied my daughter. I asked myself, "Would she have become a single mother if she had been born in a normal family?" I was breathing faintly, thinking about my daughter, who carefully kept the secret and her concern about me, her single mom who worked hard to support her. Is it worth living even if I'm unable to breathe? Would I feel the taste when I eat something to fill my stomach?

Forgiving myself was not possible. I didn't even notice that she was pregnant until the last month. I hated myself so much that I even imagined, over and over, trying to kill myself. I desperately relied on God, asking how I could even be called "mom." It seemed that neither a person nor God would possibly forgive me. I never dreamed of being forgiven.

"If you hadn't been my child . . . After spending all that hard time as the daughter of a single mother, now you too are nothing more than an unwed single mother." I couldn't believe what was happening. I was weeping bitter tears, and no ray of light was to be seen. If my husband had been there, my daughter could have gotten married regardless of her age, but that wasn't possible either. We met at a young age and he left me a long time ago without feeling any responsibility.

Worries about my daughter's future arose. Additionally, the fact that my daughter would get the cold glare of our relatives and scornful criticism of our neighbors tormented me. I felt so sorry for the baby. But I just wanted my daughter to have an abortion, even in her last month, which was actually impossible. Being afraid of some people who might know the pregnancy, I had no choice but to hide my daughter without respect to her wishes.

I was so grateful to Ae Ran Won. They helped me greatly when I was confused. Not only me, but also all the unwed mothers in the facility can truly feel thankful. Ever since I placed my daughter under Ae Ran Won's care, my life was in endless confusion without any focus. One day seemed as long as years. I got a sharp stabbing pain in my heart when I thought of my daughter. To me, it was literally a living hell waiting in panic for the baby to be born. I'd much rather prefer going insane. Finally, I got a call from Ae Ran Won that her contractions had begun. On my way to the hospital, I realized I had to meet the newborn, and it gave me great agony.

I felt so sorry and scared at the same time when imagining meeting the baby to whom I would never give a heartfelt hug. Seeing my daughter in pain, I hated the baby, who was expected to come out soon. For a while, I hated the baby so much. If I could have talked to God, I was going to blame him for letting this baby start his life in poor conditions that prevented him from receiving the proper blessings. I tried to avoid seeing the baby, but I couldn't. In fact, I honestly wanted to see him. As we were not supposed to meet again, I tried hard to put off the chance because I thought that his face would haunt me later on. However, that little baby allowed me an opportunity to see him.

My poor baby, I'm so sorry and sorry again. It is so shameful for me to say sorry to you. I'm deeply sorry, my baby. We weren't fully prepared to greet you. If I hadn't had relatives or neighbors, or if I had been able to ignore their accusing stares, I would have moved somewhere with your mom and raised you. Unfortunately, I, myself, was too immature to handle the situation.

Sweetie, please don't think we abandoned you. My life went through so many hardships and I didn't want to hand down my painful circumstances to you. I feared that you and my daughter would become miserable if both of you were living together. My baby, my heart will be burnt black with sorrow after I let you go. Even now and in the future, I cannot avoid seeing babies appearing on the TV or walking on streets.

Please don't feel that you are the only one who was hurt. We all have our cuts and bruises. I hope you grow up beautifully. How can I dare ask you to forgive your mom?

There are so many things I want to tell you, but I can't write to you any longer with my broken heart. I also wish that my daughter would not hold so many bad memories within herself all the time. I want to show my gratitude again to Ae Ran Won for providing shelter for my daughter and taking care of her.

I'm dreaming a world, where many wounded souls, like my daughter, don't need to hide themselves in Ae Ran Won anymore. I hope all the people staying in Ae Ran Won stop being sad or remorseful and live in happiness, because you can't change those things that have happened already.

Moreover, I'd like to say to adoptees: Even when you face serious and enormous problems, talk to someone around you. If my daughter had been able to talk to me about the matter earlier, we could have prevented this situation.

What would we have possibly done if we hadn't known about Ae Ran Won? I do appreciate the support we received from Ae Ran Won that helped us endure this difficult time.

PS: Our sons and daughters who were adopted, please stay in good health and love yourself in your life. With all my heart, I'm asking you to keep this in mind.

 A note from Sangsoon Han

Hee Won, the young birth mother, is a child of divorce. Her mother, Mrs. Lee, was divorced from her father when Hee Won was in the fifth grade at primary school. They have had no contact since then, so Hee Won has not heard anything of her father. Mrs. Lee raised two children while working as a waitress, but Hee Won lived at her grandmother's because her mother had to work. She finally moved to Mrs. Lee's home when she was in the first grade of middle school. But Hee Won had trouble adapting to a new school and new friends, so she ended up leaving her school. In addition, she was often physically abused by her brother, so she stayed at a friend's home when her brother acted violently toward her.

When Hee Won was eighteen years old, she was introduced by a friend to the man who would become the father of her baby. He was twenty-two years old. They dated for five years and lived together for six months. Even while Hee Won and her boyfriend were living together, her mother thought that she was still living at her grandmother's home. After she separated from her boyfriend, Hee Won came back to her mother's home. When Mrs. Lee learned from one of Hee Won's friends that Hee Won was pregnant, she tried to get her an abortion. But the pregnancy was too far along by then to have an abortion.

Hee Won learned about Ae Ran Won through the Internet, and eventually entered the facility. Her mother felt deeply guilty and suffered from the idea that she neglected her parental responsibilities. A social worker at Ae Ran Won contacted Mrs. Lee regularly, conveying messages from her daughter. Hee Won was doing well at Ae Ran Won, and hearing this caused Mrs. Lee to open her mind. She visited Ae Ran Won and had counseling with the social worker. She then went to the hospital to nurse her daughter during her labor pains.

After the baby was born, Mrs. Lee kept questioning if adoption was really the best decision. She worried that in the future her Hee Won might regret the decision. After a great deal of thought, Hee Won finally decided to give up her baby. After the baby was sent to the adoption agency, Hee Won left the hospital, but when she returned to Ae Ran Won she confessed that she wanted to keep her baby. Her mother strongly disagreed with this idea because she was convinced that both Hee Won and her baby would have trouble if she kept the baby without any preparation. She also reminded her daughter that she had a hard time raising her two children by herself as a single mother after divorcing her husband. Hee Won had no choice but to accept her mother's opinion.

She visited the adoption agency three times before her baby was sent to the adoptive parents, and often phoned the agency to ask how the baby was. Hee Won uploaded some pictures of her baby to her online blog. When she misses her baby, she looks at these pictures. One day, she was told that her baby had a heart disease. This news hurt both Hee Won and Mrs. Lee. The process of adoption was delayed slightly because of the baby's health, but finally she heard from the adoption agency that the baby was connected with great adoptive parents in the United States. The adoptive parents promised that the baby would have an operation to take care of the problem. The agency also told Hee Won to take care of herself and to think about the future, when she will meet her baby.

After leaving Ae Ran Won, Hee Won still received follow-up services such as family counseling and job education. She now has a good relationship with her brother. Ae Ran Won offered this family financial support as well. Before having her baby, Hee Won was not interested in trying to study, because they were too poor for tuition, and she felt she had no future. But now she set up a new plan. She asked if Ae Ran Won could provide for half of her educational expenses because her mother was unable to provide much tuition money. Ae

Ran Won connected her with a private school and assisted her in her studies. She finally passed the qualification examination for middle school graduation. She is studying for the qualification examination for high school graduation.

Hee Won says that she is going to enter college. She wants to present a good image of herself to her baby, so she continues to try her best, preparing for the time when she meets her baby in the future.

About Ae Ran Won

Ae Ran Won was established as House of Grace, on April 1, 1960. It began as a home for runaway girls and prostitutes. Its founder, Eleanor E. Vanlierop, was an American Presbyterian missionary who saw a need to help these young women. It was run independently by Mrs. Vanlierop, and the program was supported entirely by fundraising. Mrs. Vanlierop drew upon the love of Christ as she served unmarried pregnant women who were in need of a loving and nurturing environment during pregnancy and beyond.

In 1977, when Mrs. Vanlierop had retired and gone back to the United States, she turned the program over to the Social Welfare Foundation of the Presbyterian Church of Korea. In her honor, House of Grace was renamed Ae Ran Won. Ae Ran, which means "planting love," was Mrs. Vanlierop's Korean name.

In 1983, Ae Ran Won was recognized for its work by the Korean government and began to receive some official financial support.

Many changes and much progress have occurred over the years. In 2000, the Ae Ran Mother and Baby's Home opened, designed to support unwed mothers who wanted to keep their babies. Ae Ran Seumter opened in 2001. This group home serves adolescent mothers who have placed their babies for adoption but cannot return to their homes because of family abuse.

More recent developments demonstrate that the mission of Ae Ran Won has expanded beyond its own facilities. Begun in 2006, the Happy Mom Project, a support center for unwed single mothers who are not in one of the maternity homes, helps these mother and their babies grow in self-reliance. In November of 2008 the Happy Mom Project led to the opening of the Me.You.Us. Support Center for unwed mothers and their children who live in the local community.

Ae Ran Self-Supporting Home opened in July, 2008. Even though mothers get a job after finishing a job training course, they cannot return to mainstream society because renting a room is too expensive, and it's beyond their means in Seoul. So Ae Ran Won provides them free housing to complete their settlement in this society.

Our philosophy is to provide services that address:

- physical, emotional, financial, and spiritual needs
- decision-making about whether to parent or to place a baby for adoption; the decision to give up their babies must not be based on financial problems
- achieving self-reliance for their stable lives by first graduating from high school (or getting the equivalent degree), and then getting an employment license after finishing a job training course.

Supporting Ae Ran Won

Ae Ran Won Support System for the Unwed Mother and Child

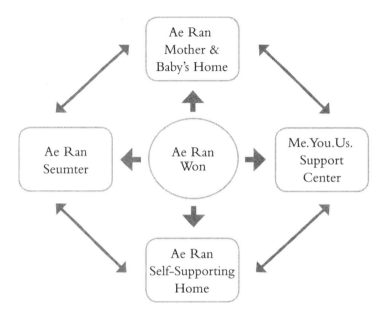

About the *Ae Ran Won* and *Ae Ran Mother & Baby's Home* logo: A mother and her baby complete their preparation for sound child-rearing and self-support. Together, they are ready to journey toward a better tomorrow.

About the *Ae Ran Seumter* logo: Having sent their babies away, birth mothers work to overcome their immense pain. In time, they develop the life skills needed to help them fly toward the future of their own choosing.

Ae Ran Won

- pre- and post-natal care
- decision-making for the baby's future
- counseling and planning for her own future
- education to prepare for self-support
- support to raise the baby

Ae Ran Mother & Baby's Home

- support for unwed mothers who raise their own children
- high school diploma or equivalent, and vocational education for employment

Ae Ran Seumter

- support for young mothers who have placed their babies for adoption
- high school diploma or equivalent, and vocational education for employment

Ae Ran Self-Supporting Home

Support and housing for unwed mothers who have their babies, and have a job, but nowhere to live

Me.You.Us. Support Center

Support for unwed mothers and their babies who live in the local community. Provide crisis intervention, crisis day care, self-help groups, parenting education, support for raising their babies; vocational education to become self-supporting.

At Ae Ran Won, we provide more than just a stable environment. We also provide counseling, schooling, and training in the skills and abilities that unwed mothers need to succeed in their lives. We know that after they leave our facilities their lives are just beginning. We are not only concerned about their lives today, but also tomorrow and the next day and every day after that.

This is why we need your help. It's often the temporary difficulties that force a mother to relinquish her child. If we can help that mother through her initial challenges, she and her baby can make a life for themselves. Right now, you can help an unwed mother and her child by making a contribution.

- $300–500 can support one mother's schooling or vocational training for a month.
- $100 (less than $3 a day) can feed a baby for a month.
- $50 (less than $1.67 a day) can buy baby supplies for a month.
- $30 (less than $1 a day) can buy a textbook for a mother's education.

Donations have also allowed us to pay for some of the medical costs incurred by mothers or babies, and also for operating the Me.You.Us. Family Center for supporting unmarried mothers and their children. In addition, donations help support three group homes and all of the additional services needed.

Owing to the increasing number of unwed mothers in need, government support is not enough. Here is a summary of our funding sources in 2008; the government support is from the City of Seoul, and the Fundraising support comes from individuals, churches and organizations.

Ae Ran Won
56% of the budget comes from government and 44% from Fundraising.

Ae Ran Seumter
The Government subsidizes the salaries of two social workers, plus 10% of the operational expenses. Fundraising provides the other 90%.

Ae Ran Mother & Baby's Home
Government subsidy 90%, Fundraising 10%.

Ae Ran Self-Supporting Home
Fundraising 100%.

Me.You.Us. Support Center
Fundraising 100%.

Privately donated funds are truly needed. While we receive donations domestically, the social prejudice against unwed mothers hinders our efforts. Therefore, we ask for your support. This is a universal problem and extends beyond borders. This is about family; it is about supporting unwed mothers and their children. Every offer of support makes a difference. We invite you to support Ae Ran Won by making an annual, monthly, or one-time donation. One gift gets results.

We would gladly have you donate. All donations will be acknowledged. There are several ways to donate, which may have changed in the time since this book was published. Please check our USA-based web site, www.aeranwon.com, for an update. Our main website, Korean language only, is www.aeranwon.org. There will also be information available at our publisher's site, www.yeongandyeong.com.

Here is the information needed to make a direct deposit into our bank account:

> Standard Chartered Korea First Bank Limited
> Account No. 300-10-047560
> *Swift code:* scblkrse
> *Account Person:* Ae Ran Won

To contact us by mail, write to:

> Ae Ran Won
> 127-20 Daeshin-dong
> Seodaemun-ku
> Seoul, South Korea (120-160)

> Our phone is 82-2-393-4723
> Our fax is 82-2-392-9933
> *(Please use country codes as needed from your phone.)*

If you have questions, you are welcome to contact me, Sangsoon Han, by email: soonhan50@hotmail.com or director@aeranwon.com. Please be sure to check our web sites for updated information and email addresses.

Thank you for anything you can do to help us.

Sangsoon Han, January 2010